THERE IS NO COUPLE

Building and strengthening bonds

NILDA CHIARAVIGLIO

For my first seeds, my daughters Maria and Ana, and for my nephew Gabriel, who taught me that children are children of life, never a private property.

To Baruch, the man I chose to build a loving-erotic relationship, to enjoy the pleasure of living and to make every minute a golden century.

Index

01

About what we call being together

& The couple does not exist, what really exists is the way in which a person is linked to another and how they affect each other; that is the **couple's relationship**, not the couple.

What we call "couple" is a specific relationship between two people, that is, it takes two adult individuals interacting under certain rules defined by both.

Life changes through time and geography (culture); today, everything is transformed more quickly due to technology; it mutates in different ways thanks to situations such as the pandemic.

We are facing an unknown world that demands a new, creative and flexible way of relearning how to relate to each other and to nature.

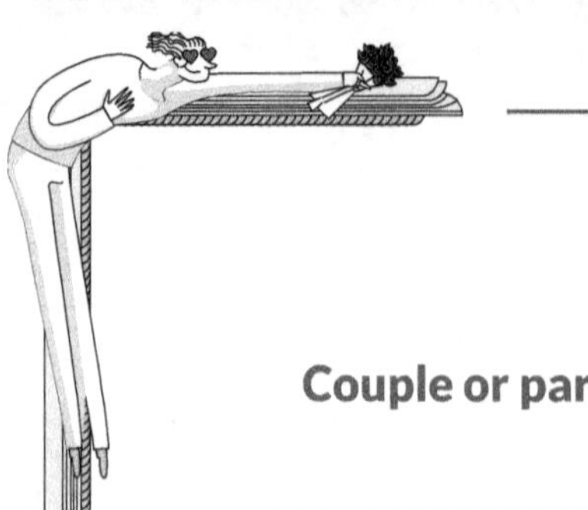

Couple or partners?

> Divorces, single mothers or fathers, people who decide to remain single after a breakup , marriages that live without communication, in conflict and violence or, in the best of cases, relationships that went from *couple* to cohabiting *partners*, parenting teammates, economic-financial convenience companions, or good friends.

All this makes us think that the relationship models that were functional more than half a century ago, have ceased to be so, in most cases. I'm sorry, but the world is no longer a Disney movie.

«There's only one thing worse than having a partner: not having one», Carl Whitaker said. Many people still think so; however, today more and more adults choose singleness and feel *at ease*, love and are loved: they perceive themselves with the freedom to do and undo their life as they please this afternoon, tomorrow and in the future.

Relationship models fall like statues of old tyrants, and one of the heaviest is patriarchy.

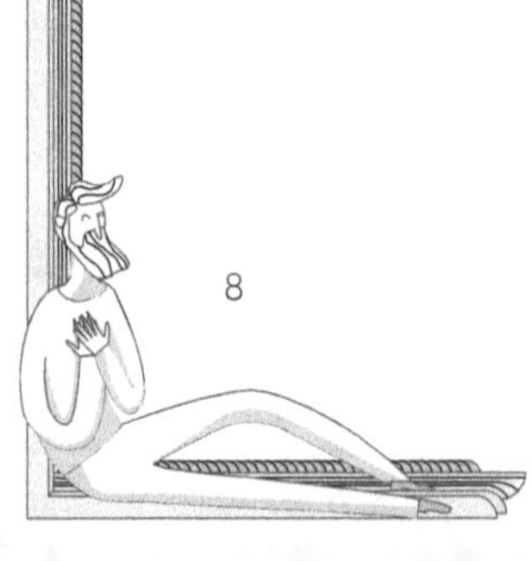

Nilda Chiaraviglio

   Dear Carl, the world is flooded with people who think that there is only one thing worse than not having a partner: having one.

These adults, who build new ways of relating, share their free time, their travels and their sexuality with others who have similar life goals, will always find another human being who wants to share a good *plan* with someone independent and free from the commitments of a loving-erotic couple.

   Today, chatting with acquaintances or strangers is considered to be an excellent plan when deciding to stay at home, not to mention the video meetings that we inherited from the Covid-19 pandemic. Nothing as simple as swiping right or left on the **smartphone** screen, inside a dating app.

Love in evolution

In any of its forms, from those practiced in African savannahs thousands of years ago, to those customary in our days, love has taken and will take infinite forms of expression.

& We are biologically loving beings, for love has been our central emotion for millions of years.

Life is like that

As a result of our decisions, we get feelings or situations that disgust or hurt us; however, that never means that we are *wrong* or bad, or, in the worst case, «that our life has been a mistake».

We have to reflect again on what were the behaviors that have brought us to where we are, what variables we forgot to take into account, which we did not contemplate enough and from what beliefs we made such decisions.

This gives us the opportunity to use the first freedom of the human being: to change course, to decide again what to think, what is appropriate to have the life we want and get where we want.

& We build our existence according to **how** we think and feel.

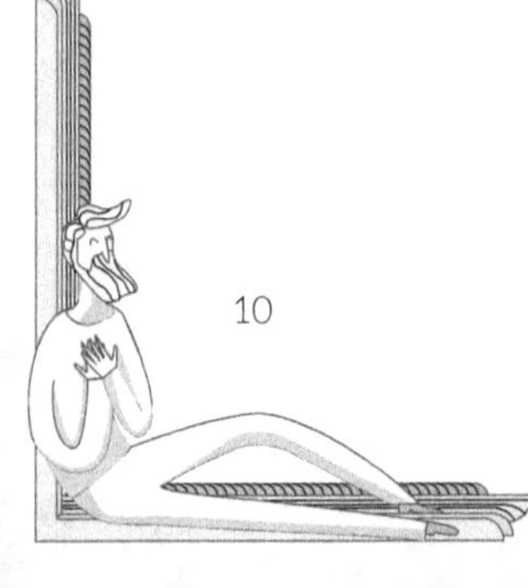

They say that we are all unique and unrepeatable and, for better or worse, it is true. Our interpretations of what happens in the world and within us depend on our life history, what we reflect on and what we decide to transform in order to adapt our beliefs to reality.

It is always possible to change

If we analyze our lives – with their pains and dissatisfactions – from a loving perspective, with the desire to understand the positive intention that each of our decisions had, without judgments or punishment, we will find the path to what we need to modify in order to be well.

 & Each person defines what it is to «be better» according to their own criteria, education, desires, interests, values and tastes.

A behavior that works great for someone may be a very ineffective strategy for someone else, or it is possible that something that worked for a long time may lose its effectiveness; even a successful action tends to lose its luster under certain circumstances.

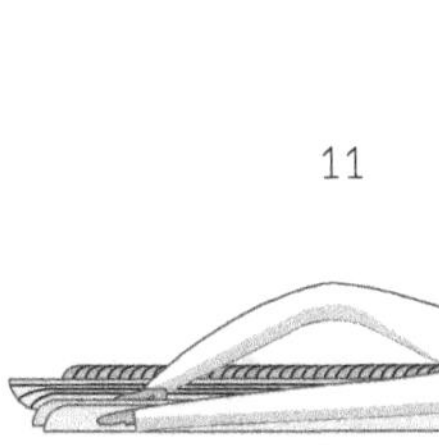

When we have enough resources and skills to manage our lives, it means that we have already developed the right flexibility to take responsibility for our well-being.

& It is impossible to change others, but we do have the power to transform ourselves and our relationship (the fifty percent that we're responsible of).

Learn to enjoy

It is important to enjoy love, freedom, health, sensitivity, material privileges, equity, abundance, nature, history, art, etc. It is very likely that thanks to these pleasures we learn how to make the right decisions to attract more of that and make our life and partner a wonderful masterpiece.

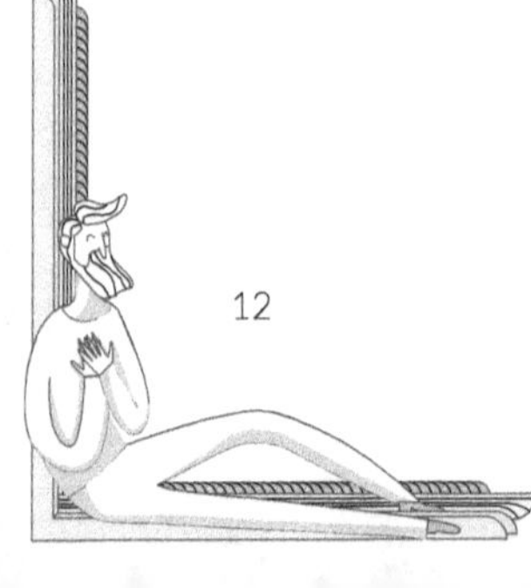

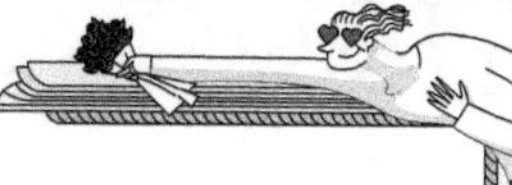

> If we live focused on looking at "what is missing", on what others do not do or do wrong, complaining about our partner andthe world, we will stop enjoying everything we **do** have and we will waste the power to build our well-being.

Paradigms

We can think of a paradigm as a set of ideas that explain «the way of living and life itself.» We constitute and reproduce them as if they were viruses for which face masks and sanitizers are useless.

> Our behavior is the result of the order that our brain gives when it is exposed to any stimulus, that is, from *something* that happens *outside* (reality) and that is captured by our senses, or from *within* (beliefs).

This behavior responds to the interpretation that we build from our *software* or life history, and that constitutes a filter formed from experiences.

Our way of thinking is built by all the rules, beliefs, uses and customs that we have *bought* from who knows from whom, and without having the slightest idea of what they're for.

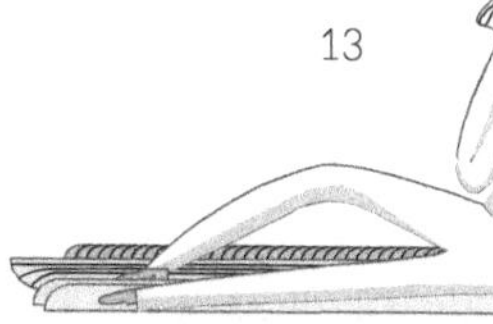

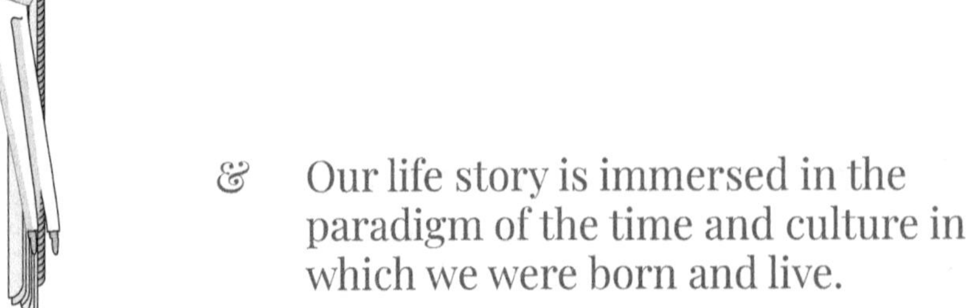

  Our life story is immersed in the paradigm of the time and culture in which we were born and live.

Today, East and West, North and South have blurred their borders, generating mixtures with complex and dynamic balances, almost as immediate as clicking on a web page.

We wake up, meditate Zen-style after a half-hour yoga session, have breakfast while on Zoom with a friend in Paris, have lunch with our partners in a Chinese restaurant and have Italian food for lunch, watching an Indian-produced film; throughout the day we listen to music from all latitudes and on TikTok we watch videos made by people of all skin tones. This seems natural to us.

  However, we keep wondering why Romeo and Juliet's romantic-love-erotic relationship model works poorly or weirdly for us.

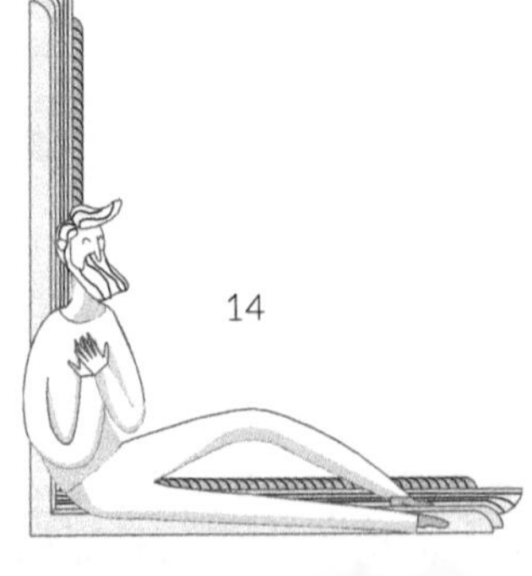

PARADIGMS
of human relationships over time:

Before the year 1500
Phenomena without an explanation are blamed on God or the Devil.

XVI and XVII Century
Separations: God of science and mind of body. The division of labor leaves women in a lower hierarchy.

XIX Century
Aspiration to economic and material advancement. Classes control the paradigm (oops: patriarchy).

XX Century
The change in values is evident, which allows the discovery of potentialities unknown to minorities.

When the paradigm shift moves from science to the social context, the fear of losing power over others deepens existential crises.

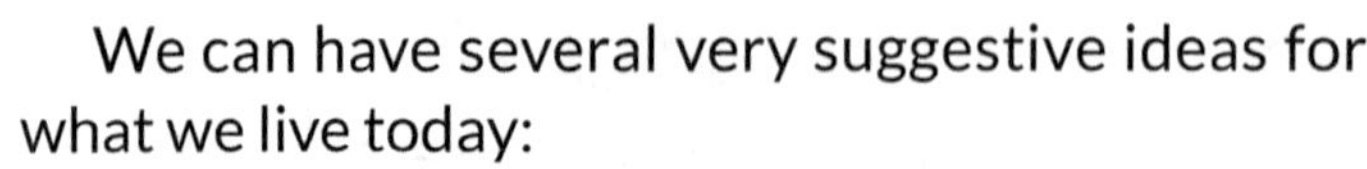

We can have several very suggestive ideas for what we live today:

- *We evolve from the need to explain the mysteries of life and to solve the suffering caused by ignorance.*

- *Every paradigm contains the seed of its own destruction.*

- *The difficulty in changing paradigms is based, among other things, on the fact that the belief system is inadequate to perceive the changing reality.*

- *The fear of losing what you have, even though it is not very functional, generates barriers to change.*

- *The separation into parts of any event, and of individuals, is actually non-existent; we are a network of indivisible interrelationships.*

- *It is the whole that determines the behavior of the **parts**.*

- *Absolute truth is non-existent.*

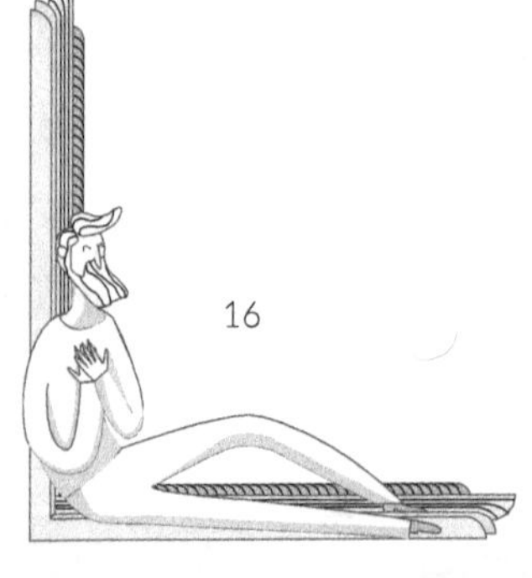

Nilda Chiaraviglio

- *The world depends on the way we observe and narrate it.*

- *People who dare to think with different rules, with critical and countercultural thinking, generate new paradigms.*

- *Human consciousness is at the center of any study.*

& The paradigm determines the behavior of the human being.

A Silent Death

We are experiencing a process of cultural death that is the incubator of a new paradigm: **the silent revolution of the counterculture.**

This death and resurrection is the cause of the explosion of all the voids that are generated in society, which does not change its paradigms to the rhythm of «existential longing».

It is interesting to discover that an important part of our current culture continues to reason to the beat of the SIXTEENTH and SEVENTEENTH centuries; for example:

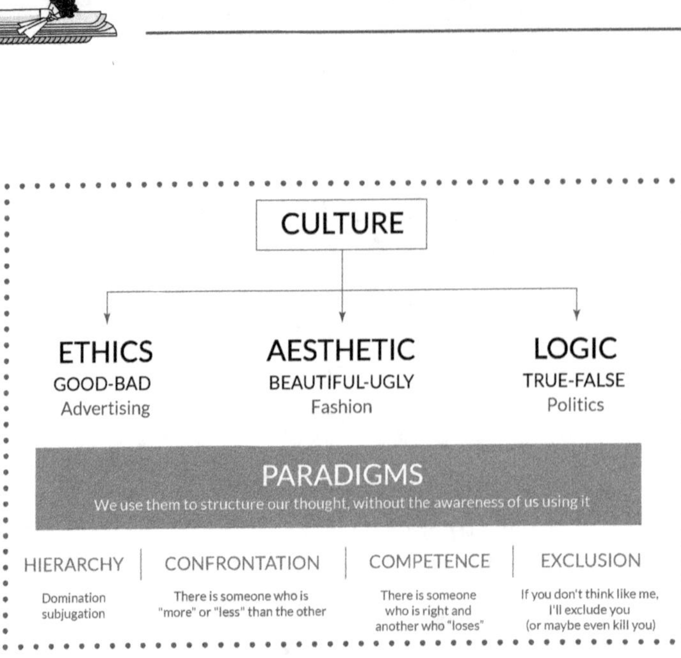

Love is still conceived in terms of the bond between separate entities.

*The fantasy of **security** is still obtained from the feeling of possession.*

The exercise of power is done in terms of separate hierarchies.

*The illusion of **control** is executed as dominance over others or over **that** part of oneself.*

Fidelity in a couple is lived as a physical behavior, separated from biological reality, mind, commitment and emotions.

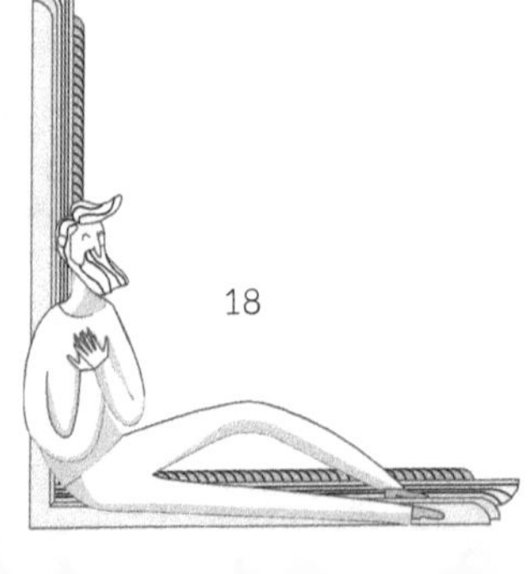

Nilda Chiaraviglio

- *The feminine is perceived as separate from the masculine as a gender role.*

- *Economic abundance is built as a result of the destruction of nature.*

- *The personal point of view is exposed as absolute truth; everyone believes they are right and own the truth: «If you think differently from me and it was impossible to convince you, then it is **valid to** attack you».*

- *The perception of God is that of a being separate and above us, who distributes punishments and rewards (what about free will?).*

- *Hierarchies are defended through weapons, wars and the destruction of nature.*

No, the world is not one of those who shout the loudest.

The four *paradigms of the Apocalypses*

Culture has imposed on us prototypes that carry symptoms and consequences that arise from the belief system that we inherit.

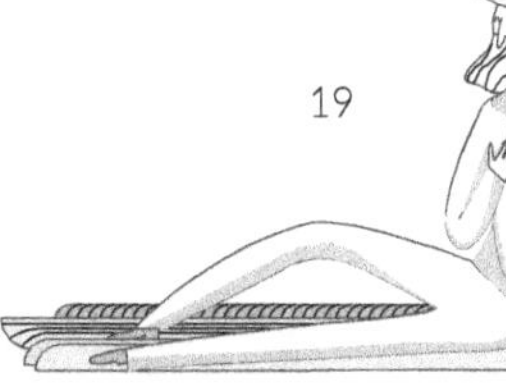

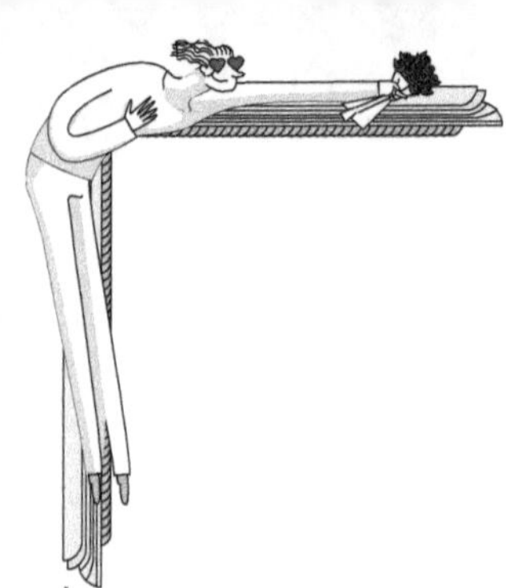

THE FOUR PARADIGMS

Culture has imposed prototypes consequences that arise from the

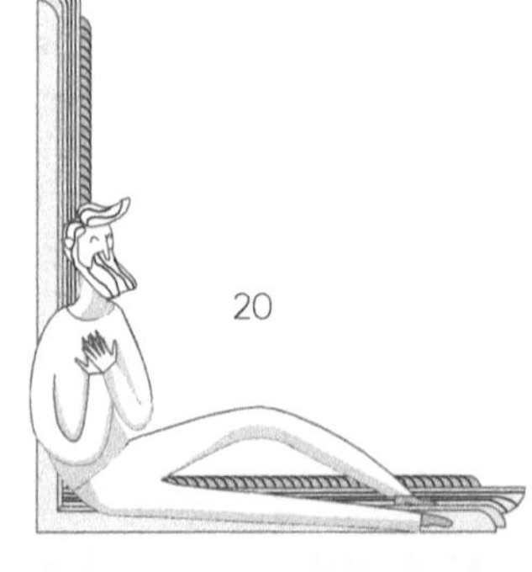

Nilda Chiaraviglio

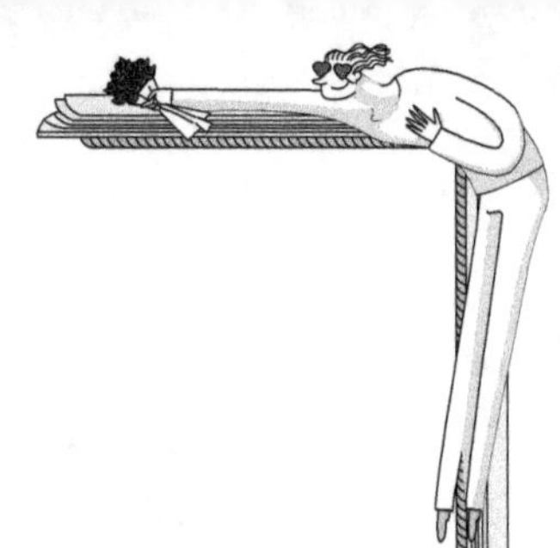

OF THE APOCALYPSE

on us that carry symptoms and belief system that we inherited.

Are you aware of how much you have inherited from previous models? Do they generate conflict, violence, control or jealousy, guilt or shame? Do you feel able to set loving and firm boundaries based on those beliefs?

&   Do you take responsibility for your individual well–being, or do you expect others to do the work?

What is the model of man-woman that you have? A handsome, seductive, good provider, kind and loving man to his family, while bold and successful on the outside? An educated woman, always willing to support her husband's plans and desires (erotic as well) and take care of the household (children included)?

&   Is this how you want to spend the next twenty years? How is your Apocalypse going?.

Conceiving ourselves separately gave us the opportunity to become aware of the importance of interpersonal relationships.

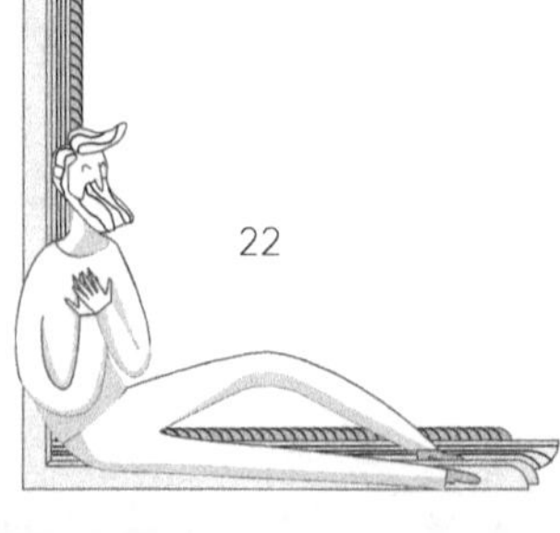

W e demonstrate the inability to establish nurturing human relationships, turning the capacity to love into a *thing*, into a *cheese* that, when distributed, decreases and, therefore, you have to fight for a piece of someone's love and then possess and control it.

Love is neither a cheese nor is it bought; it is a decision about how to expand the capacity to love with which we are born.

Uncertainty

We are facing a change that will imply a re-education of the human being as an integral part of the **whole**. This transformation forces us to review the concept of a couple from different points of view.

We can think that there are many and very varied definitions of «couple» because it is a term loaded with meanings and variables.

E. Morin speaks of the couple **rescuing** the concept of "human uncertainty" as something inherent in the human being. That gives us an interesting explanation to understand why most of us seek to live within a loving-erotic relationship, as if dying alone was something unnatural.

A long time ago, the couple (man and woman) was

important for the reproduction of the species, but today that is no longer a problem (we are more than seven billion human beings on this planet); however, we continue determined to making emotional commitments.

> It is the gaze of the other that confirms our existence as beings different from all others. As they say in the film *The Incredibles*: «When everyone is super, no one will be».

By building the mental unit called «couple», the human being manages to put under (relative) control the uncertainty of the mystery of life: its appearance and its disappearance, through the rules, controls and restrictions that a relationship entails.

Uncertainty imprints on people – and, therefore, on the couple relationship – a central characteristic: fighting all their lives to feel *safe*, although from somewhere in their unconscious they know that the human being lives in (with and from) uncertainty all their life.

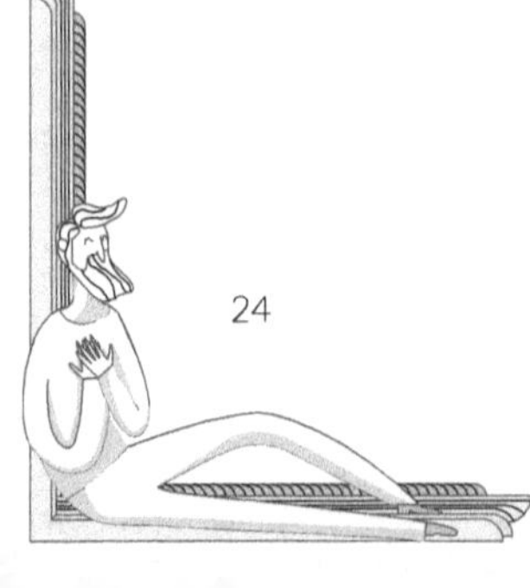

Bored?

R. Manrique argues that, to the extent that the human being builds a network of beliefs that increases his sense of security, he will be able to move away from the idea of mortality, then the anxiety and anguish caused by uncertainty decreases, therefore, boredom also increases and erotic desire decreases.If that happens, it is very likely that crises will appear in the relationship.

&   The antidotes to boredom are naivete, curiosity, spontaneity and communication.

There seems to be an inverse function between boredom and the anguish or anxiety of living; we seem to like danger, as if the mere risk of being alive were not enough.

The illusion of acquiring the *security* that posessing a person grants has been sufficient motivation for most to look for that other human being whom they will call a partner (or maybe a crutch in the face of uncertainty?).

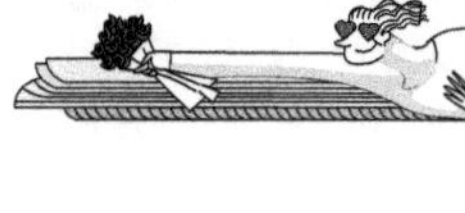

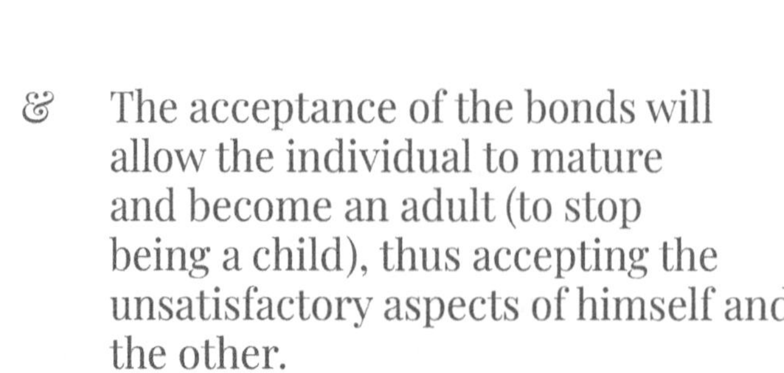

  The acceptance of the bonds will
allow the individual to mature
and become an adult (to stop
being a child), thus accepting the
unsatisfactory aspects of himself and
the other.

> That image that many people bring to the consultation of «I am fine, the other is fine, but the couple is wrong» is imposible, because if the couple is what is wrong, it will be necessary to review what are the behaviors of the members that compose it in order to reflect on what are the variations that each of them needs to make.

Growing up and maturing implies a greater degree of awareness and, therefore, an increase in the anguish and anxiety caused by our existential conflict.

  Everything that allows us to feel
«more alive» and with less conflict
involves learning to handle doses of
variable uncertainty versus doses of
security.

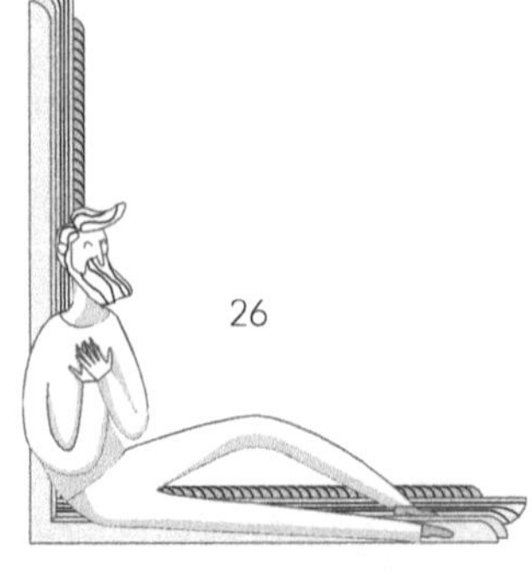

   Nilda Chiaraviglio

02

Love and butterflies

& Loving and being in love are totally different things.

Falling in love has nothing to do with love. Butterflies in the stomach are usually a gang of liars. Relationships are neither sought nor found: they are built over time and with time.

LOVE	BEING IN LOVE
Is a choice, a decision	Is a feeling.
Involves actions	It implies a thrilling emotion
Two adults are needed	With one who falls in love is enough
Leads to an erotic love commitment	Is transient

TO LOVE AND BEING IN LOVE
Are totally different things.

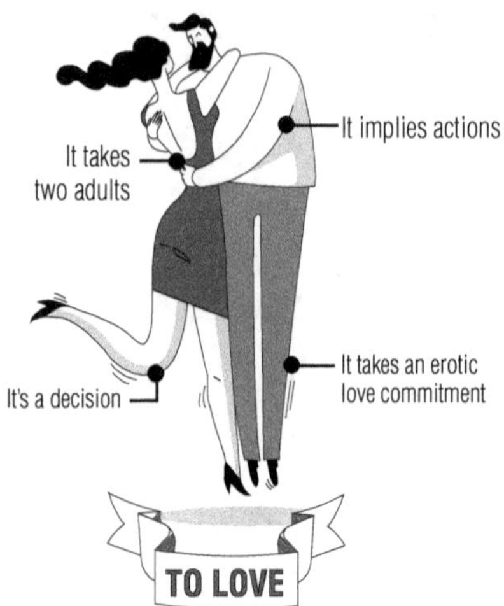

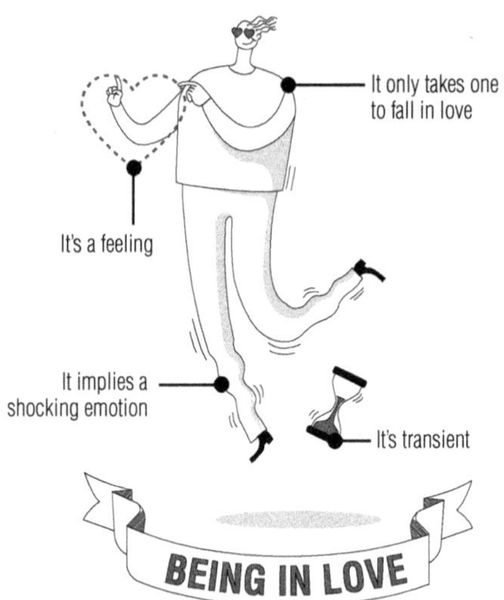

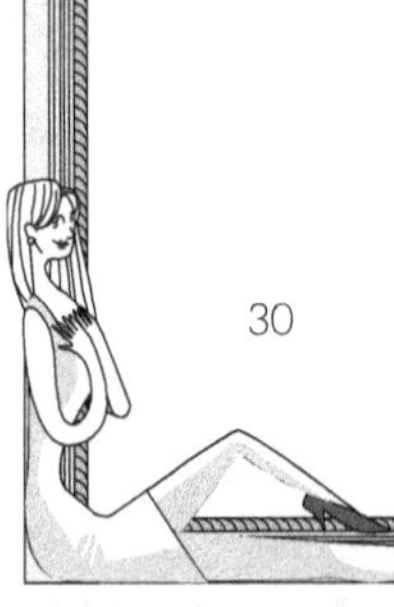

Nilda Chiaraviglio

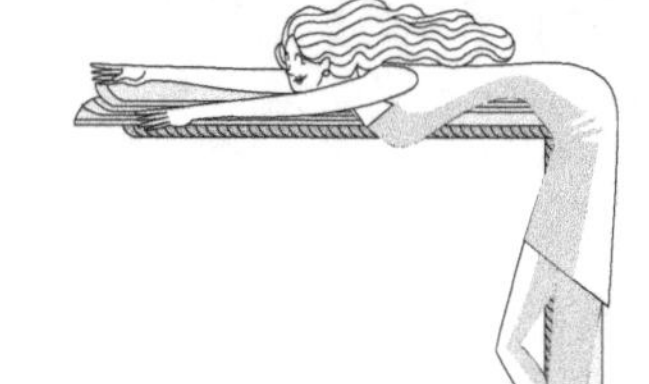

Crazy for you

The feeling of being in love is a night with fireworks, a feeling of renewal, creativity, fantasy and kindness.

& The eyes of the person who falls in love distort the vision of the world and of themselves.

We have all had that romantic movie experience in which we believe that the borders between us and the other are being erased, that we know each other without restrictions, that full surrender floods us with harmony in the geography of a world formed for both.

Sounds cheesy, doesn't it? Of course, and it's because during that period of falling in love psychological processes occur in which people see, think and feel the same; they even evaluate reality in a similar way.

& In another context, these symptoms could be defined as «mental disorders».

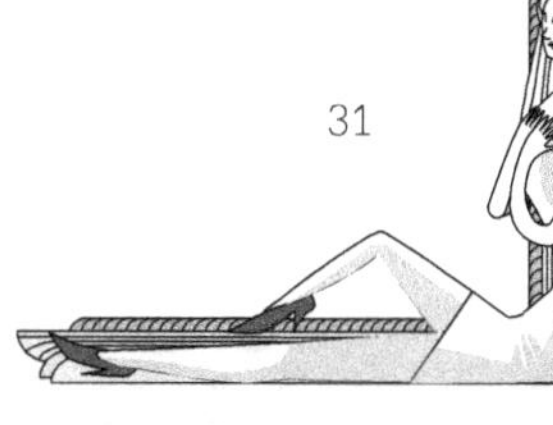

Mirror

Falling in love is selfish, because one is enraptured with the best that the mirror of our perception returns to us and, in this process, sees in the other an idealized reflection.

Although we think that the person with whom we fall in love with is very different from us, there are always common denominators: interpretations of the world, shortcomings, anxieties and defenses that come from childhood and seem to define us.

Why so much madness?

Whoever falls in love, suffers, is out of balance, even gets depressed, presents anxiety, as if he were in a prison of uncomfortable circumstances; however, that emotion gives them strength to face the revolutions of the world.

Falling in love is like an energy drink that gives people strength to make decisions, take paths and

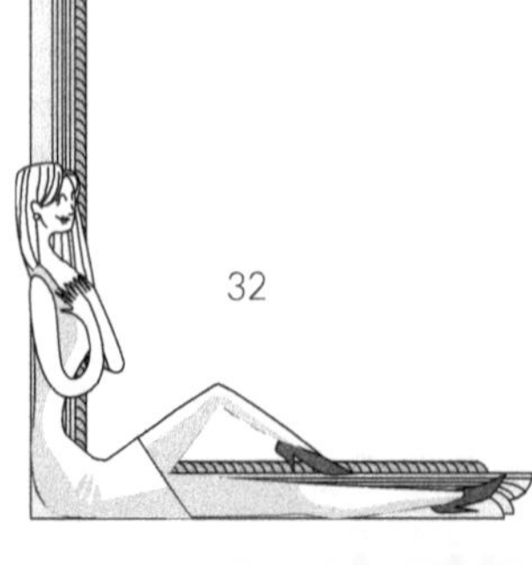

Nilda Chiaraviglio

draw curves. That's why it's more common during adolescence and in the *crisis* of the forties, that is, ages that represent turning points in the human experience.

The fulfillment of cycles, such as job, social or personal losses, a significant move, the end of a career, etc., are circumstances that attract the experience of falling in love.

When we are young, we think about who we're going to share that vital impetus with, and when maturity comes, it fills our heads with questions about where we will make our final nest, even if there is still a long way to go. During the period of falling in love, or infatuation, we create pleasurable versions of the past, present and future.

The end of the story

The emotion breaks down when the mirror fogs up and that fairytale image appears unknown: denial disappears, we see the stains and Cinderella's carriage transforms into a Halloween pumpkin.

The loss of identity is always lurking during the period "falling in love" and this entails the need to

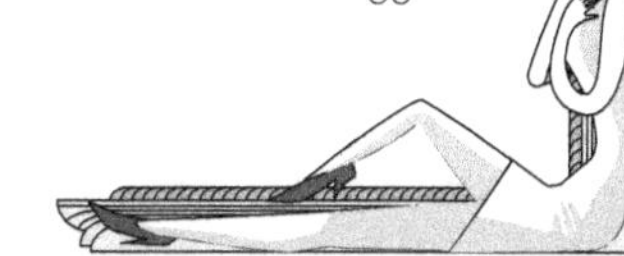

mount a defense; the differences between the couple – which had always been there – increase, because things look different, in a selfish way.

> Falling in love is very unstable, it is a situation that evolves towards love, towards hostility, or towards a breakup.

During this period of infatuation, there is always a threat of loss of individual definition, which creates a lot of anxiety, and with it, the need to build a defense. The difference with the other begins to be considered as something bad and this is how our personal identity feels safe.

& It seems like a paradox: while experiencing the best in ourselves, the worst appears.

At the end of this emotion, the distortion of the reality of the other and the partiality of oneself, vanishes. The bridges that communicated the identities of the couple become unsustainable and the unity ends, which is usually difficult, painful, full of disillusion and disappointments. The hope of that New World withers.

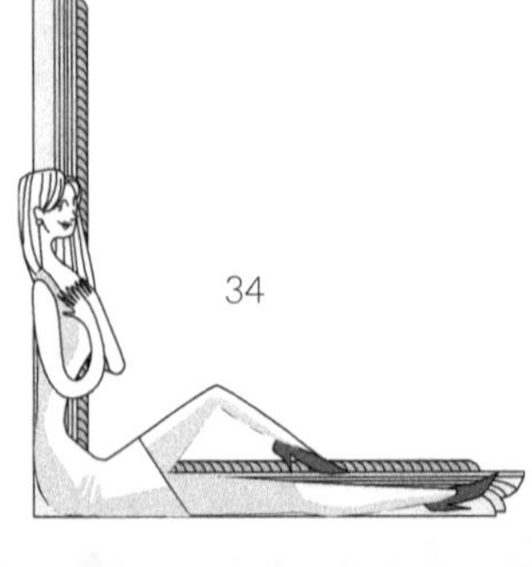

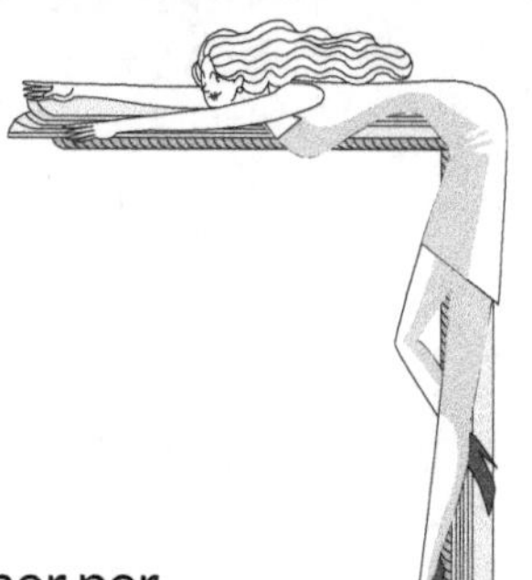

The hangover after falling in love

Heartbreak feels almost physical, as if the other person were ripping us to pieces and we, at the same time, were scratching and tearin out their skin.

During infatuation, the prefrontal cortex of our brain produces an unusual amount of oxytocin, and this hormone fulfills the saying that «love is blind.» We become the cheerleader of a memorable binge.

Oxytocin has a limited time to enter the celebration of neurons, then, they close. The party lasts three years at most — sometimes three days — some studies say, although psychological changes are faster.

Infatuation also releases endorphins, which make us feel better physically and emotionally. When the perception of having been in *heaven* is diluted, the decrease of this neurotransmitter is a resounding visit to the ground.

&   If two people decide to get married immediately, it is very likely that the feeling of falling in love will disappear. If you're in love, do NOT get married.

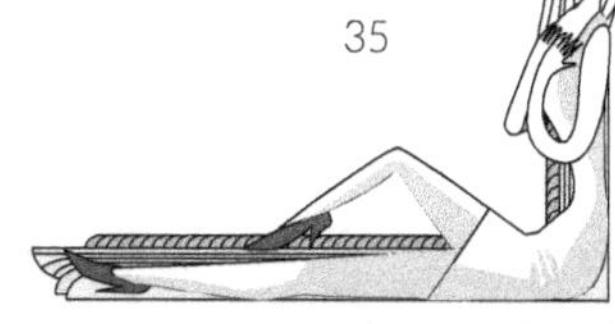

Solo emotion

Sometimes, love is not reciprocated and falling in love becomes a crisis by not finding the love object.

> & In order to fall in love, you don't need two people.

When someone does not interpret the other well, their infatuation is one-sided. If that someone decides to turn to another person as a way of forgetting themself – because they do not tolerate their own story – they fall in love without being reciprocated.

The most complete and complex way in which two human beings can be linked, is love, and love is an internal and subjective relationship. It takes two people for it to happen. Love is not like falling in love, which can exist on one side only.

Infatuation can also be confused with sexual desire, great admiration, gratitude, guilt and even hatred. There are other feelings that pour into a relationship and create the «erotomaniac delusion,» but that always has an inevitable end.

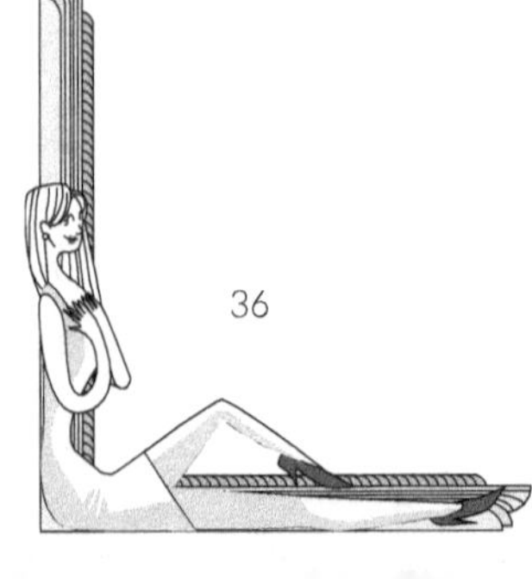

Nilda Chiaraviglio

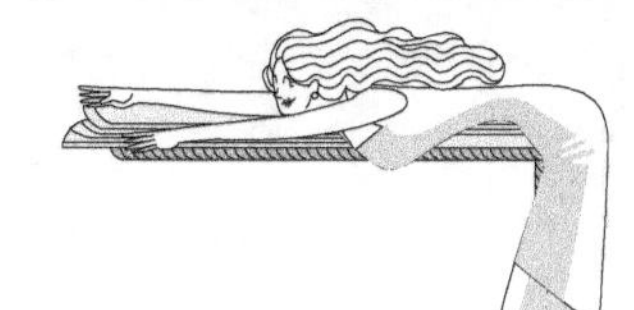

Love

The idea of oneself in the other is unified in love: we are individual beings capable of building a different character to be able to love: it is necessary to assume the other.

Choosing someone involves dealing with the doubt of what life would have been like if another decision had been made. These doubts can be cleared up in the real love relationship, without losing the individuality of those involved, and embarking on a common path.

&   To love» is a verb, a behavior, a capacity that develops towards infinity.

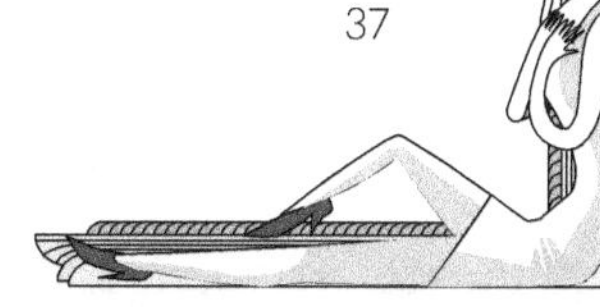

Finite Love (from Romeo and Juliet)	Love as an infinite capacity
Relationship as private property, full of magical thoughts.	Relationships with growing individual freedoms.

Unlike falling in love, love is a conscious, personal and free act. It is impossible to love someone who does not love us. The most common characteristics of love are:

- *Care, concern and occupation for who we love.*

- *Accepting that the other is part of our life.*

- *Respect for the individuality of the other.*

- *Understanding the other is using their own codes.*

- *Attraction, desire and pleasure.*

- *Eroticism. The actualization of the past*

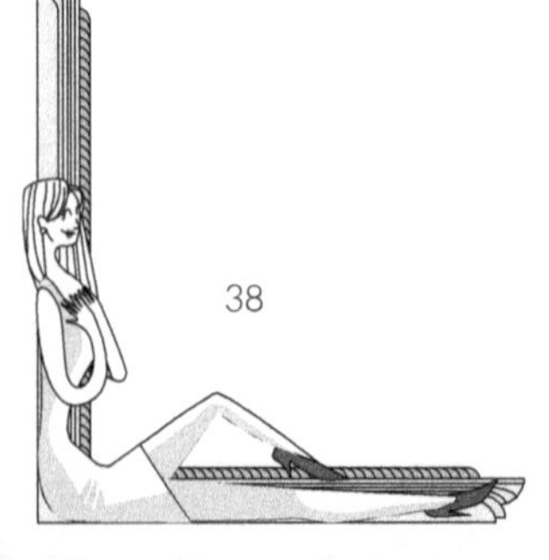

Nilda Chiaraviglio

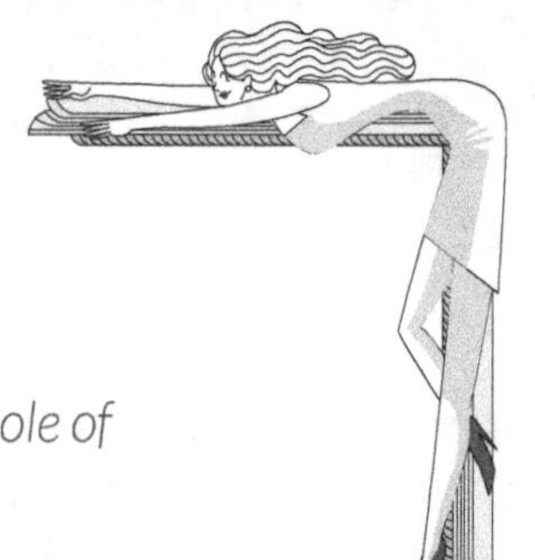

with all its fantasies, revives the whole of each person's existence.

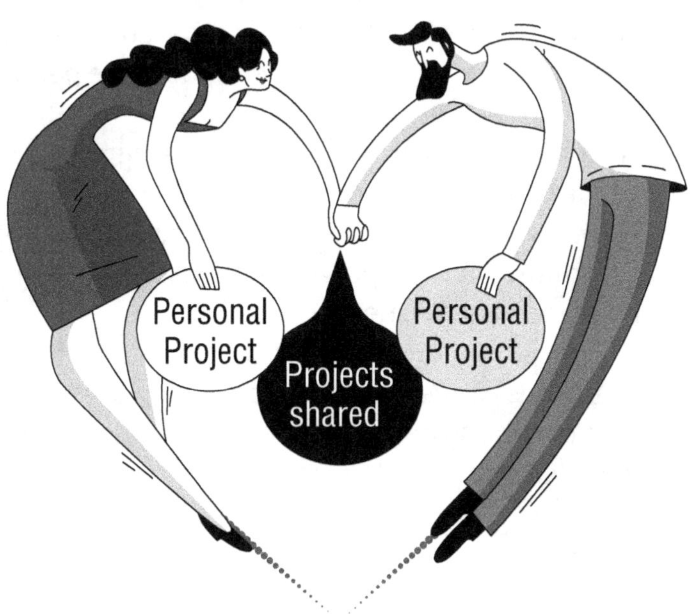

• *It seeks a model of relationship, a bond independent of any child models.*

• *Dynamic balance so that difficulties are transformed into agreements.*

Conceptions of love

The idea of love and the emotion of love are two different things.

Idea	Emotion
. It is a social construction inherited from the TWELFTH century at the service of reproduction and the consolidation of that system.	. It is present in all human beings naturally.
. It changes according to the culture.	. It arises from the action of loving. There are as many different ways to love as there are people.
. Romanticism separates men and women.	. It allows acceptance.
. It divides women into wife (submissive) and lover (erotic).	. It builds reciprocal and compatible relationships.
	. It promotes the pleasure of being together and integrating freely.
	. Violence disappears.

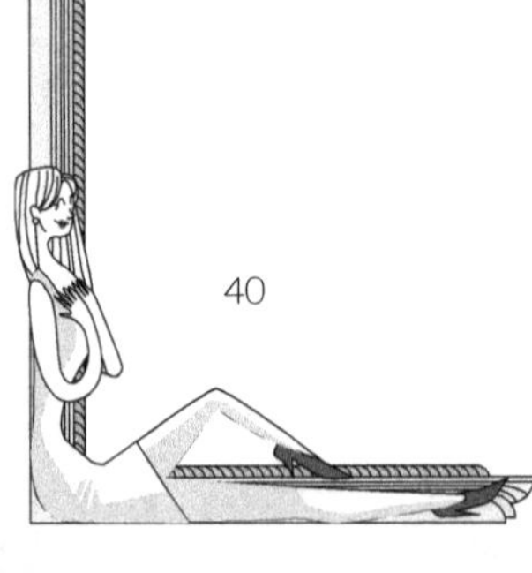

Love is central to the preservation of our human identity in a committed, active, intimate and erotic relationship.

> The couple relationship is useful in the construction of an individual project of each person, it is alive and evolves with the circumstances of life. The objective of the relationship is the subjects that compose it and not the relationship itself.

If two people have personal projects, and between them, they have other projects in which they share **V**alues, **I**nterests and **D**esires (VID), then it is likely that the vital space of the couple relationship will increase and strengthen.

The more individual projects grow, the more the couple's project can grow.

Falling in love is always on the tightrope: it evolves towards love or turns towards hostility and the end of the relationship.

When people start feeling less and less free, because they have a partner who controls everything they do, at what time and with whom they go out, what they wear, etc., a feeling of suffocation begins, as if the power goes out from the bedroom and jealousy was a toxic gas that kills individuality.

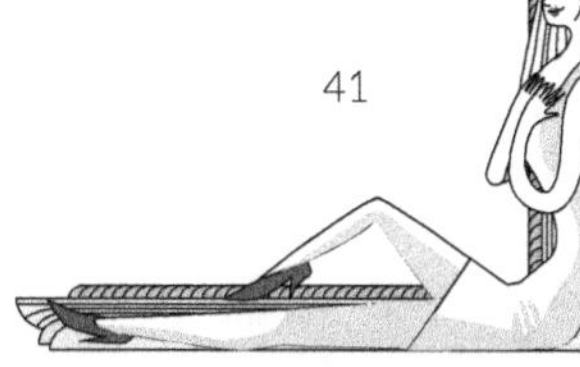

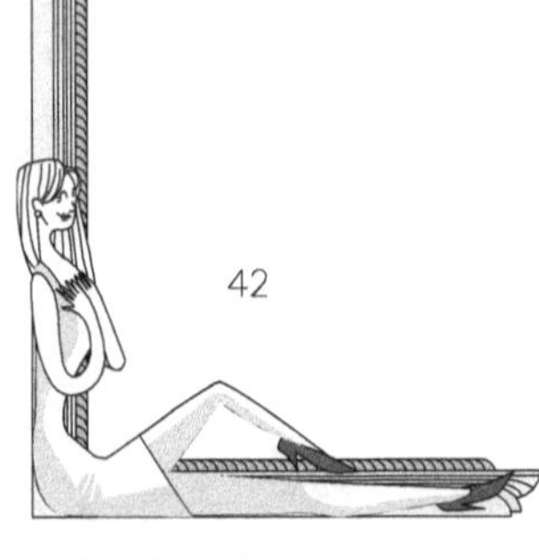

Nilda Chiaraviglio

03

I, in love, am an idiot

& It's time to forge a custom-made model.

If you are starting a relationship or throwing a life-line at someone who is drowning in a gigantic glass of water, you surely have many questions, and of course you are under the spell of traditional models and family education.

Imagine that, because you want to and can, you buy a helicopter, without even knowing how to fly it, you get on it and intend to see the city from the sky. A bit idiotic, right? Similarly, how could a person establish a loving-erotic commitment, without first knowing what style and quality of relationship they want, what they like to give, and what they like (or choose) to receive? Well, it happens all the time.

Disappointed couples often come to my office: they decided to be together and it turns out they never really wondered how they were going to get organized; they both believed they wanted the same thing and that they would live «happily ever after.»

When two people come together, the word «The End» does not appear like in the movies, on the contrary, everything is just beginning and, the more self-knowledge they both have and the more explicit their agreements are, the better.

&   For coexistence as a couple to be pleasant, it is necessary that each one feels respected and encouraged to develop their dreams, Values, Interests and Desires, (VID).

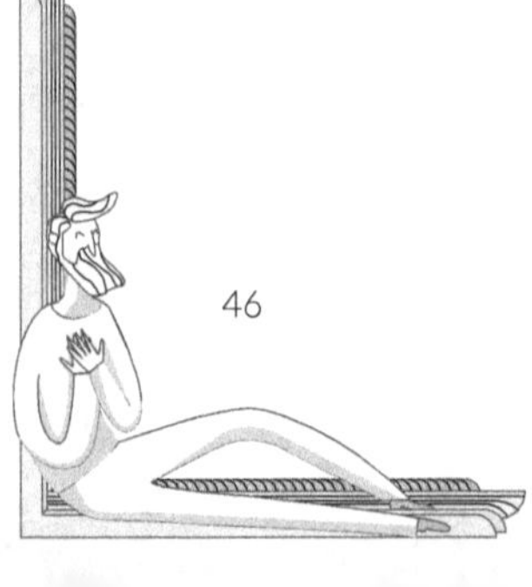

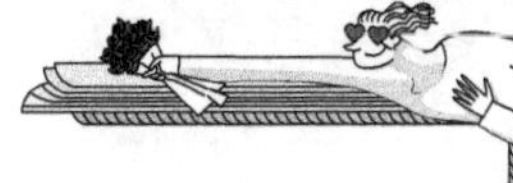

Red flags

To those *who were left* without a partner for whatever reason, I ask: what do you choose or decide? Many are paralyzed, staring into infinity; they know what they dislike, but few are clear about what they do like or want. One word: **self-knowledge**.

In some cases, the most evident upset in a couple is the fatigue of living in conflict and, in extreme cases, in emotional and physical violence. Boredom also tends to arrive, they both feel lonely, there is a lack of erotic desire ... anything is a good excuse to wear a long face throughout the day.

There are some people who believe that «everything is fine», means living comfortably together, being well organized, with shared plans, communicating with affection and respect, being independent and great friends, but at the same time, they have a red alert at the erotic level.

&   Each couple has a unique problem
     and the way of evolving is particular,
     with its own times and forms.

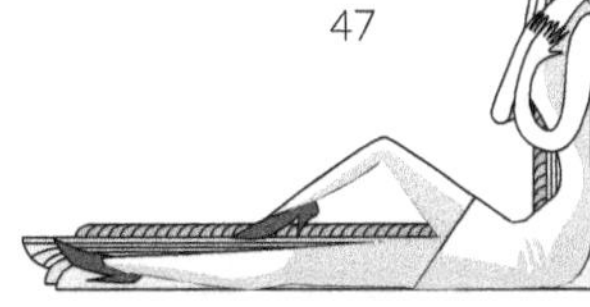

The dilemma of change

Any transformation has a price that generates con-sequences in the relationship.

   People seem to cling to the behaviors that make them suffer, even if they give them *security*; they also interpret the actions of the other without asking if their deductions are true or just part of their imag-ination, even if that invention causes them pain. For example:

> *He didn't call me because he didn't care, or maybe something bad happened to him. Maybe he had to do an unexpected job, or just got delayed buying flowers for me, or maybe...he went to the supermarket, or he's with someone else...*

& What's going on? Why suffer unnecessarily?

The dilemma of change consists of reflecting on how to find paths towards a new relationship, paying special attention to the connections between the members of the couple:

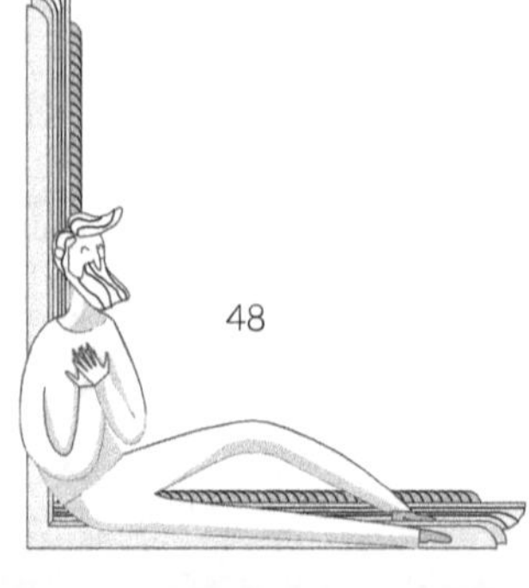

Nilda Chiaraviglio

Each member of the couple can only be understood in the context of their totality.

The change of one affects the other.

The parts are constantly transforming to maintain balance.

Each uncomfortable situation is considered important as a particular case.

The shape of a couple depends on the bonds weaven between the parties.

&   No one person has unilateral control over another. The balance is in the continuous organization.

The couple is a system in which there are no absolute terms or certainty; every action affects the whole and the parts.

Transformation is not a single solution to a single problem, but rather a dilemma to be solved. Any modification pays a price and raises questions:

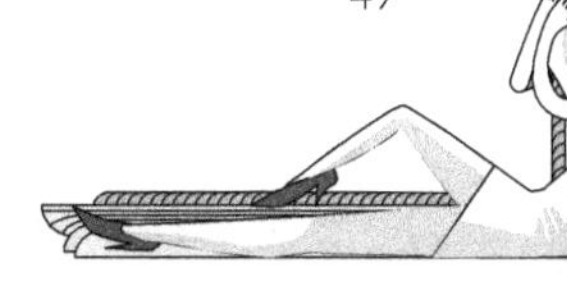

- ❦ *What will happen if the problem is removed?*

- ❦ *How will the couple work without that problem?*

- ❦ *What price should be paid for its elimination?*

- ❦ *Who will pay for it?*

- ❦ *Is it worth it?*

Relationship problems

The conflicts of one of the members are transferred to the couple, no matter who caused them and how to eliminate them. That is why self-knowledge of both parties is so important to discover the belief system from which decisions are made: attitudes, basic assumptions, expectations, prejudices, convictions and ideas inherited from the families of origin.

It is very common to find couples with the expectation that the only one who has to modify things is the one who feels *bad*, and many times

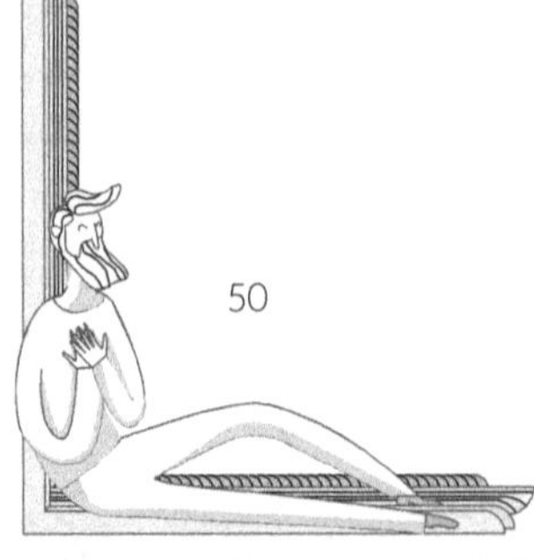

Nilda Chiaraviglio

that is the case. However, even when that person resolves what is affecting them, the relationship will be transformed because that person will be putting a different behavior in the bond than the one both were used to.

The first step to achieving evolution is to understand that a certain discomfort involves the entire system called «couple». Some key questions to find that out are:

- *Why is this problem presented at this very moment?*

- *What are the events and behaviors that have caused the problem?*

- *What are the events immediately before, simultaneously and after?*

- *What cycle of interaction is keeping it in place?*

- *How has this cycle been changing?*

- *How has the couple's method of dealing with the problem been modified?*

- *What effect does it have on each of the parts?*

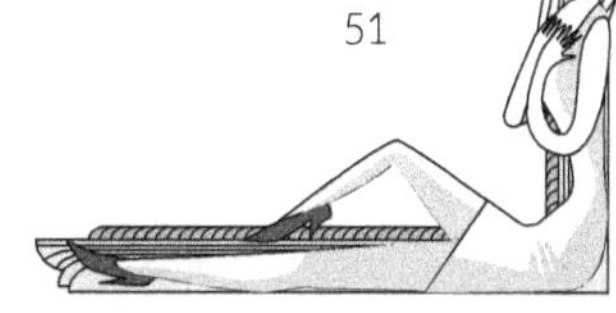

- *What will happen to the couple if the problem persists?*

- *...and what will happen if the problem goes away?*

- *What role does the symptom of conflict play in the destabilization of the couple?*

- *How does the couple work to achieve stability?*

- *What is the central issue around which the problem is organized?*

- *What kind of feelings does this problem generate and how are they expressed?*

- *What anxiety around this change activates conflicts that have been latent, and these, instead of being resolved, are expressed through a symptom?*

- *What is the influence of families of origin on this problem?*

Working as a couple

Complete the following chart to assess your relationship with your partner, so that you can clear any doubts about whether your situation is nutritious for you or not:

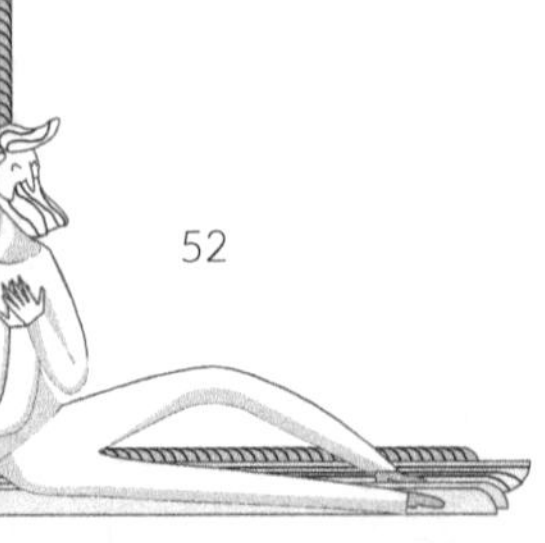

Nilda Chiaraviglio

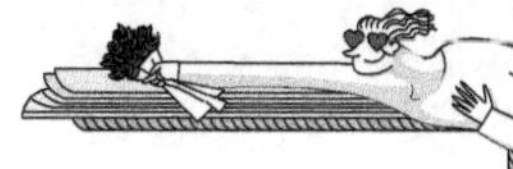

IF I SEPARATE FROM MY PARTNER	
What do I gain?	**What do I lose?**
1	1.
2.	2.
3.	3.
4.	4.
...	...
n.	n.

After writing down your thoughts and reflections, rate each one from 1 to 10, in the columns at the ends. 0 means that it is of no importance to you whatsoever, and 10 means that this is very important in your life.

Add both columns. Look at those numbers and see what you feel if they're high or low:

- *Do you gain more than you lose?*

- *Do you lose more than you gain?*

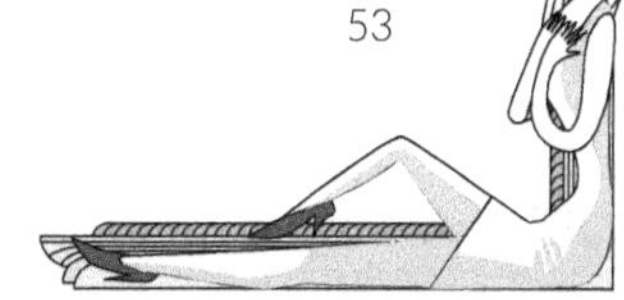

& What does that mean to you?

A single person can perform the above exercise based on their own definition of what it is to be committed and decide if they prefer to continue like this or review with what type of person they would be interested in building an affective relationship.

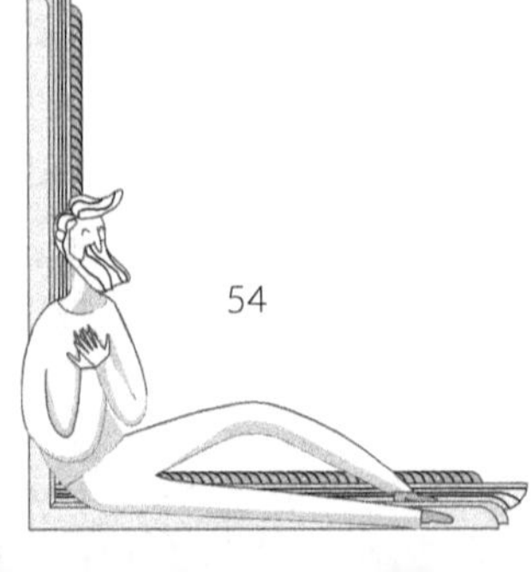

Nilda Chiaraviglio

I love

An efficient strategy for self-knowledge, focused on establishing or improving a relationship is to ask yourself: how do I love when I love? What do I do when I say I love? By what actions do I show that I am loving?

When we talk about love, we assume we're being clear and that, in addition, *loving* is the same for everyone. But each person has their own way of *loving*, which, if it were not enough, is transformed throughout life.

&   Love in our 20s is different from the one we express at 30, 50 or 70 years old.

If, for me, calling my partner's cell phone ten times a day means *loving her*, and it turns out that she feels loved if she only gets one call a day (the others are interpreted as persecution), then chances are we will have a problem.

You love

The other side of the coin also raises a question: what would I like to happen (out there) to feel loved?

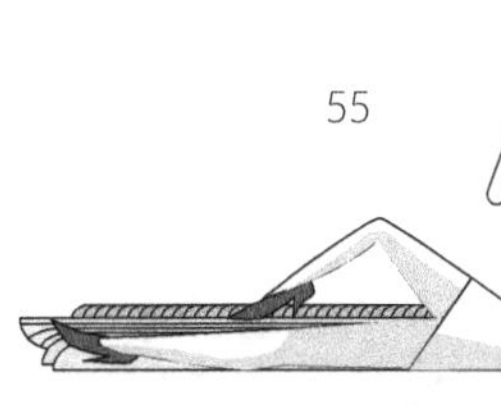

& Every human being feels loved only if certain things happen, or the other partner does or stops doing a specific something.

If we are clear about the attitudes that make us feel loved, we can choose a partner who includes those characteristics in their way of showing love, and can only be achieved through **self-knowledge**.

> Being informed of what we can expect from the other and what will never come from them will allow us to make decisions about whether that is really the person with whom we want to share our life with.

How do I know I love?

This is just one example, you could build your own list:

- *I respect everything I like and what attracts me to my partner.*

- *I accept what I dislike, and I put adequate distance to respect, understand and comprehend those aspects.*

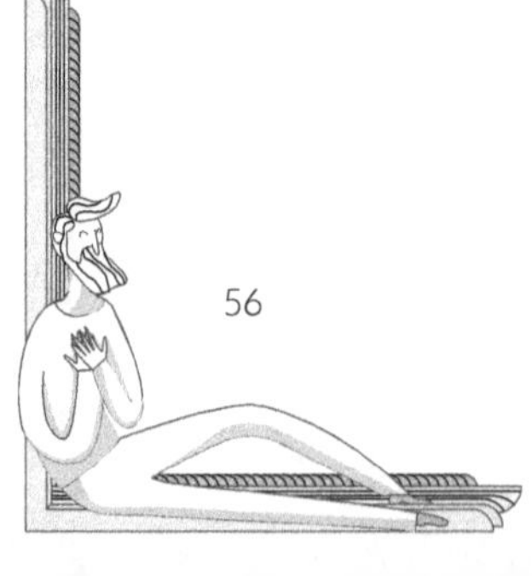

Nilda Chiaraviglio

&a; *I embrace the other as a being in permanent transformation and enjoy putting one more feather on their wings every day.*

&a; *I prepare a surprise for them that I know they will like.*

&a; *I call or send them messages at the **agreed time**.*

&a; *My partner makes me curious and I want to learn from them.*

&a; *I have the disposition to contain and take care of them.*

&a; *I enjoy giving them what they like, if I have it at all and it's good for me.*

&a; *I can receive and ask for care and attention without fear of collection and without creating expectations of it happening.*

&a; *I am never afraid of judgment when expressing my doubts, confusions and shadows.*

&a; *I rejoice with their joys and accompany them in their pains.*

   I desire erotically, I enjoy hugging them, kissing them, caressing them, looking into their eyes, absorbing their smell and taste; I enjoy melting into their body and soul.

   Sometimes I feel like we are one.

   It gives me pleasure to know that the other knows themself free and shares their freedom with me.

   I leave the doors of my life open for them to come in, stay and leave when it's good for the other and for both.

   I listen to new ideas because I know they will never hurt me and I propose new things.

   What do I want to happen in order to feel that they love me?

I feel loved when:

   My partner respects, enjoys and promotes my freedom and my transformations.

   He listens to me with curiosity and interest.

   I can ask for something with the certainty

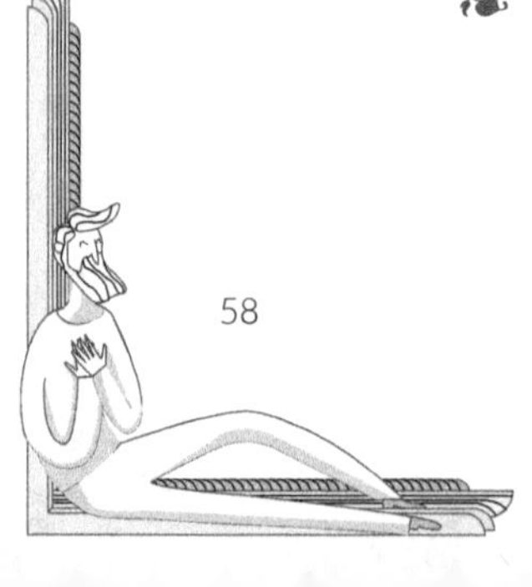

Nilda Chiaraviglio

that he will only give me that which is good for him and for both.

ɷ   *He trusts my abilities and accepts my decisions, even if they are changing.*

ɷ   *He proposes me to create and widen the space of intimacy and eroticism.*

ɷ   *He calls me or writes to me as we have* **agreed***.*

ɷ   *He looks with respect at the worst of me and accepts it as a part that I still have to illuminate.*

ɷ   *My partner can say no, without fear.*

ɷ   *He respects my private spaces.*

ɷ   *He feels happy with my happiness, my growth, my dreams and my ideals.*

ɷ   *Together we seek humor, curiosity, optimism, joy and faith.*

ɷ   *Differences enrich us.*

ɷ   *He takes care of my pains and sleeplessness.*

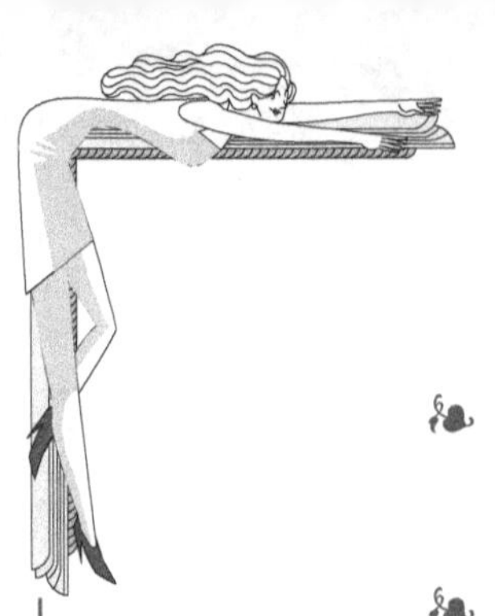

- *My weaknesses and strengths are embraced equally.*

- *He allows me to repair mistakes from a place of honesty.*

- *He exercises the right to privacy as something sacred, but never opens a distance between the two*

Propose to your partner to write, separately, two lists similar to the previous ones, without consulting each other. When you both believe that you have expressed your thoughts, I suggest that you perform the following exercise:

- *Person **A** reads his list of **How Do I Know I Love?** and person **B** searches and marks on their list of **What do I want to happen to feel loved?** those points where you both coincide.*

- *Now, change roles and do the same.*

Surely there were unchecked points in the two lists

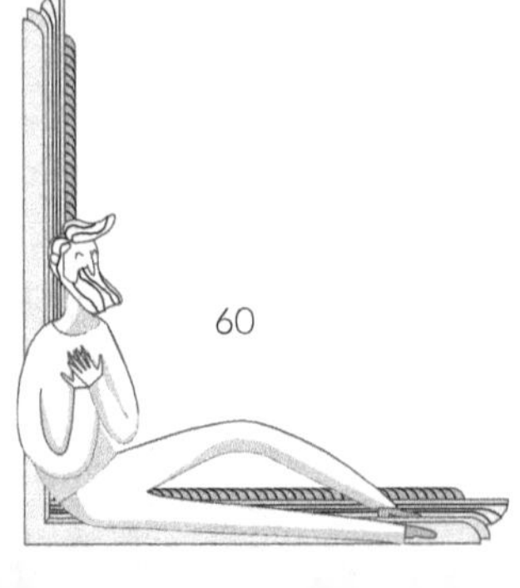

Nilda Chiaraviglio

of what you want, so talk about what behaviors you would like to perform so that the other feels loved. There may be several points to agree on, but try to cover them all.

People are amazed at how little they know themselves and their partner, but after this exercise it is easier to make the other feel loved, although the most important gain is that both become aware of what are the elements to build their relationship.

& Now you can say, "I, in love, stopped being an idiot" or at least, a little less.

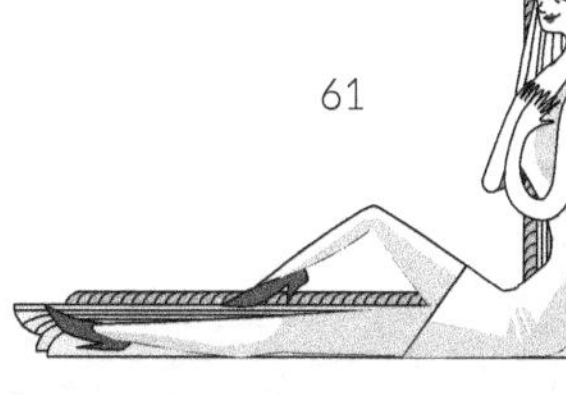

The parties
transform
constantly to
maintain
balance.

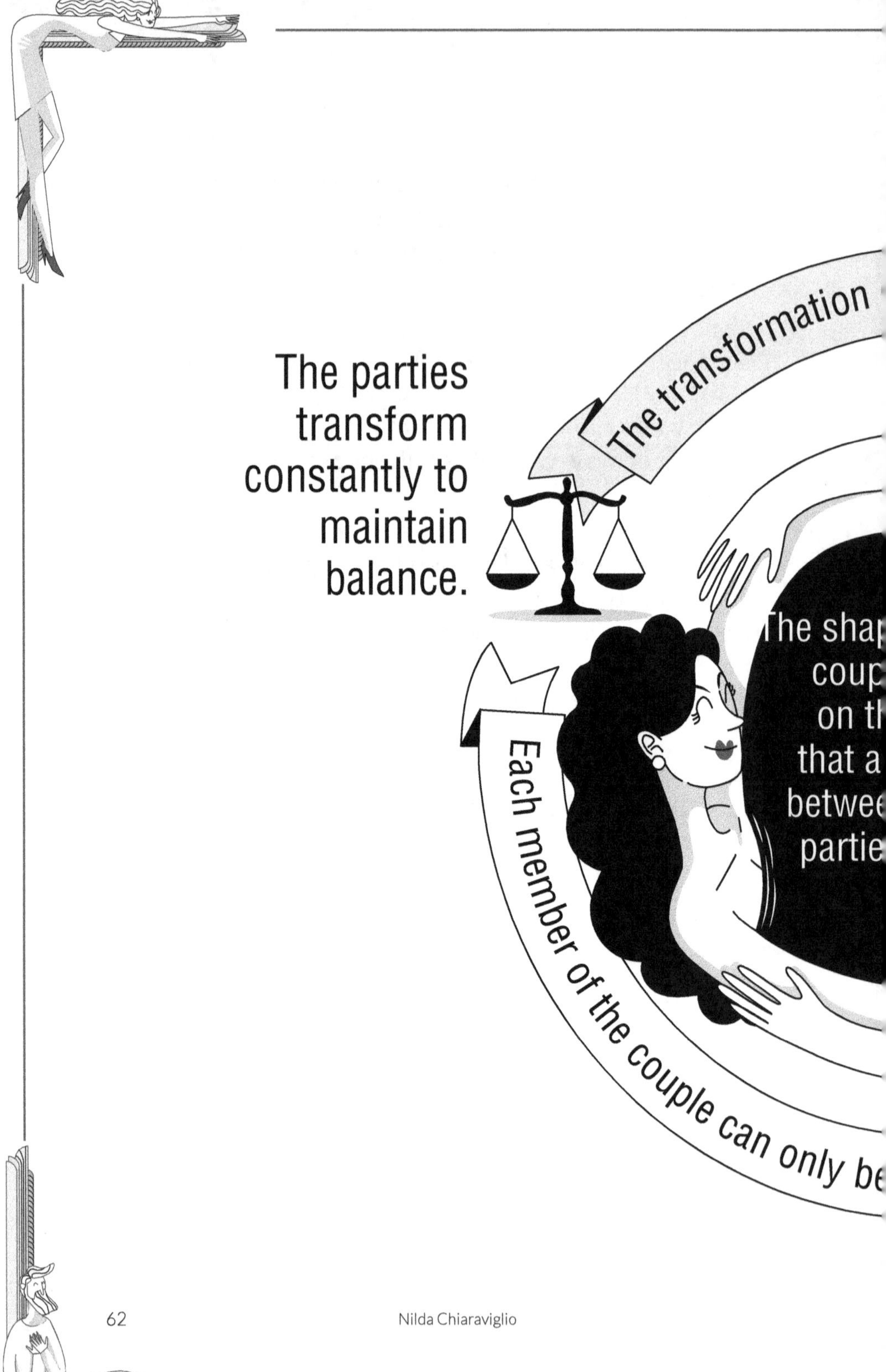

Nilda Chiaraviglio

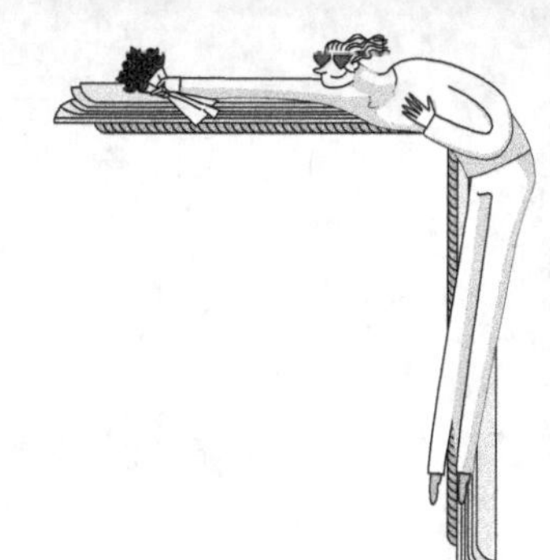

e affects the other.

f a
epends
onds
oven
e

understood in the context of his totality.

Every uncomfortable situation is considered important as a particular case.

04

Like and dis*like*

What do I like and what do I dislike about the human with whom I share life? Admittedly, there are always certain characteristics we won't like about a person, relationship, or situation; the important thing is that each member of the couple asks themselves what it is that they dislike about the other. Sweet things are obvious, they always produce a special sparkle in the eyes, but bitter ones can be a complicated subject.

I suggest you do the following exercise:

	What I like	What I dislike
She		
He		

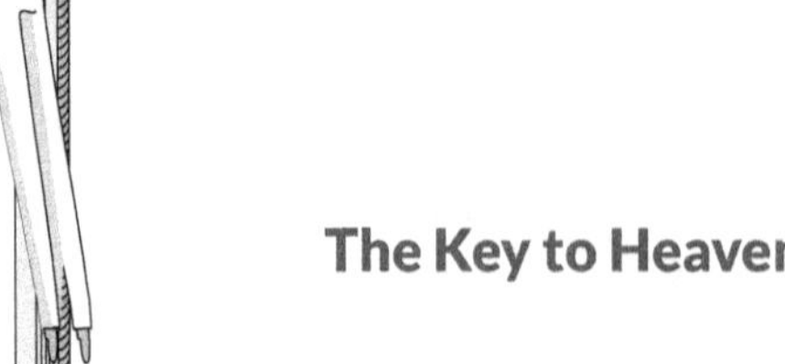

The Key to Heaven

If I am the one who has a problem or discomfort, it is precisely me who will have to solve it and never leave my well-being in the hands of another.

The key to heaven is a useful tool for smoothing *rough edges* and «opening the gates of paradise.»

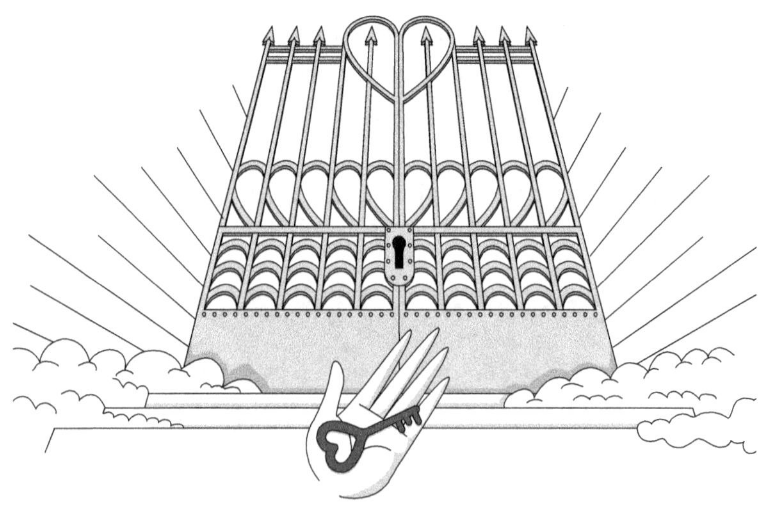

First Gate of Heaven

Whose problem is it? Whoever feels it.

If I am the one who experiences disgust, annoyance, pain, anger or discomfort, the problem is mine. If it's the other feeling bad, the problem is theirs.

Second Gate of Heaven

Who can solve the problem? Whoever has it.

The intention of this exercise is to restore peace to the relationship; opening these doors represents a satisfactory way out of the conflict, because, if the problem is mine, I am able to do with it what I think is right and good.

> & One of the most serious obstacles in conflict resolution is feeling that my well-being is in the hands of another person or external circumstance.

When both members of the couple find out whose problem it is, they can follow the next sequence:

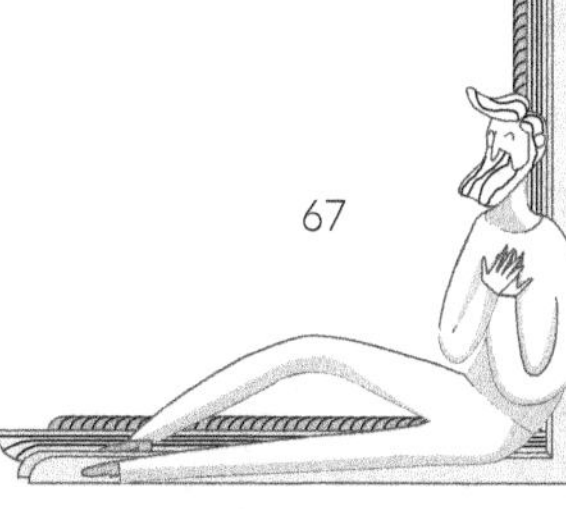

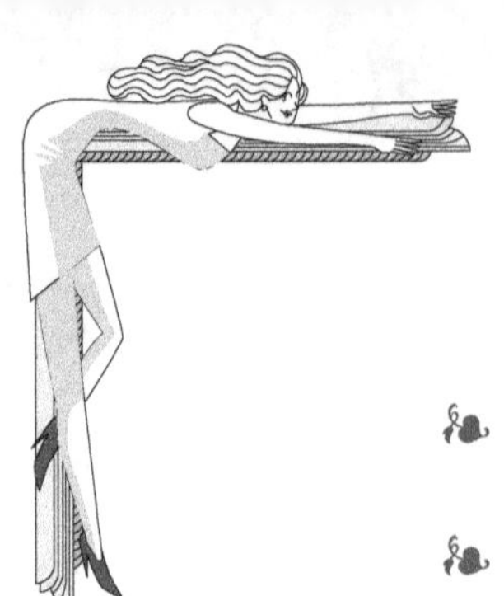

Finally, reflect and find **together** the resources so that whoever presents the discomfort resolves it; that is, not because one of the individuals presents the problem, they must be left alone: remember that the couple is a complex piece of machinery, and that the conflict of one affects the whole.

With this tool both lovers are usually relieved, because one assumes that their discomfort is theirs and that they will solve it in their own way, and the other is comforted by not carrying unpleasant matters or external issues anymore.

When each one takes responsibility for solving their discomforts, the affective bond is strengthened.

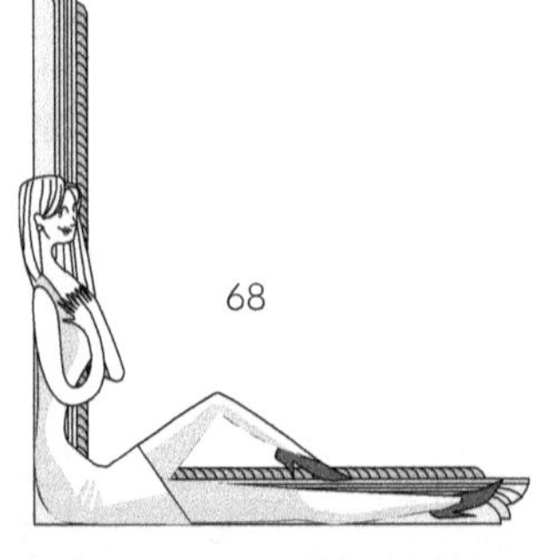

Nilda Chiaraviglio

No *like*

Perhaps one of the members of the relationship will have a harder time going through the whole process; the level of difficulty depends on the **self-knowledge** of each one, on knowing how we love and how we feel loved. For example:

> *He tells her that he is very upset that she calls him so much on the phone and asks him who he is with, what he is doing, where he is, and so on; that it makes him feel controlled, angers him and drives him away from her to the point of not wanting to see her.*

Many would think that she has to stop calling him so much; however, the one who feels the discomfort is him. One suggestion is for him to ask himself if that happens to him especially with her or if he feels that way with other people.

Most likely, it is a nuisance that appeared before he met her. If so, it is useful to search the memory for the first memory he recalls having had that feeling and work to remove the meaning he put on it, then he can agree with his partner on a new communication system with the information they need to organize their activities.

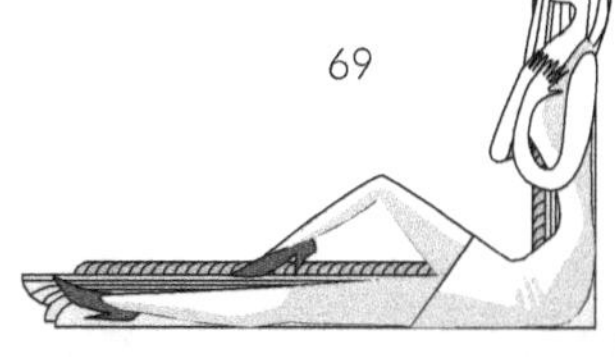

What I offer and what I like to receive

What is the couple model I prefer? What could I offer my partner? To solve these questions it is essential to turn once again to our old and reliable companion: **self-knowledge.**

Let's do an individual task so that each member of the couple to question and lay the foundations to forge mutual agreements or to start a new stage of the love-erotic relationship.

You can add or remove concepts according to your interests and way of life, as it is an individual exercise. I always recommend keeping point 1: «What is love?», since it probes the possibility of talking about the difference between infatuation, romantic love – full of magical thinking – and real love. I advise that the following topics are focused on trust and romance.

> We call magical thinking to the act of waiting for something to just happen («we will be happy ever after», «love can achieve anything», «I will make you happy», «I cannot live without you», and so on) knowing that this does NOT happen.

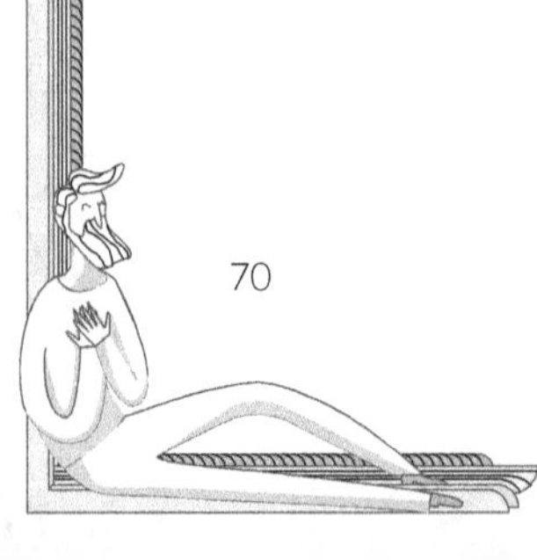

Nilda Chiaraviglio

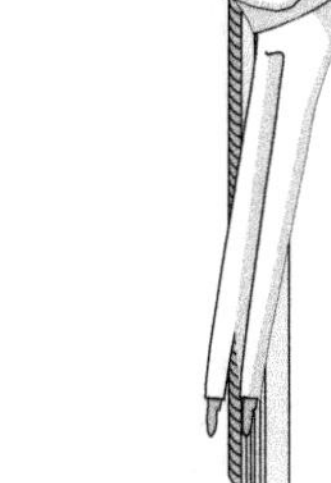

	What do I think?	How do I feel?	How do I act?
1. What is love?			
2. Trust and jealousy			
3. Romanticism and real love commitment			
4. Money and management			
5. Sexuality and seduction			
6. Work			
7. Family and friends			
8. Physical and emotional health			
9. Leisure time, sports, travel			
10. Children			

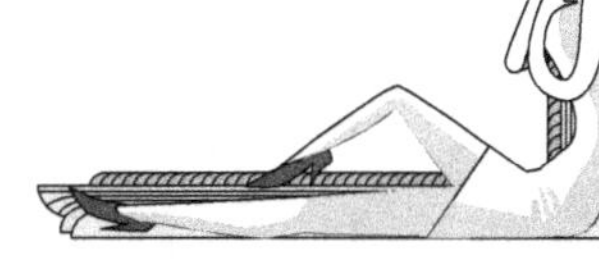

Once you have elaborated the previous exercise, which helps to raise individual concepts about love, trust and romanticism, ask yourself openly:

- *When you met, did you fall in love or just became friends?*

- *Have you ever fallen in love?*

- *When did you decide to start loving each other?*

- *What were the differences between feeling in love and starting to love each other?*

- *Did sexuality change between you?*

- *Did you indulge in romanticism when you were in love or when you started loving each other?*

- *What romantic activities did you practice in each stage? What did you achieve with them?*

- *When did you begin to feel confident?*

- *What did the other person do to make you realize that you had started to trust?*

- *Are you both usually trusting, or is it especially with the other?*

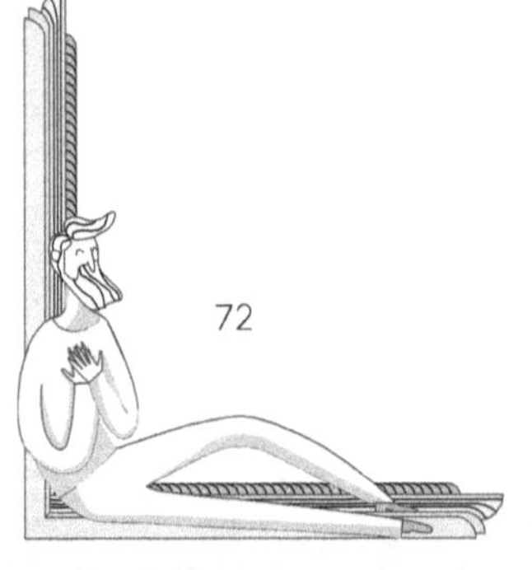

Nilda Chiaraviglio

Do you have any idea when or how trust started and developed?

Let's make a deal

When a couple is disappointed, hopeless and in crisis, a reflection can be made using the expectations they had in the beginning and the possibility that the relationship can give them to develop their individual desires and tastes.

Often couples come together without reflecting on the concept of love or how a relationship is built; they simply do what tradition or culture indicates. This is called **implicit agreements**.

When lovers talk about how they love, how they want to be loved, their Values, Interests, Desires (VID), sexuality, infidelity, etc., and reach agreements that are suitable for both, then we can talk about **explicit agreements**.

An agreement is very different from a negotiation, because the latter it is achieved by thinking on how to win, and it is fragile.On the other hand, an agreement is achieved by having an open dialogue, so the result in not only better for both, since it's very pleasing, but also lasting.

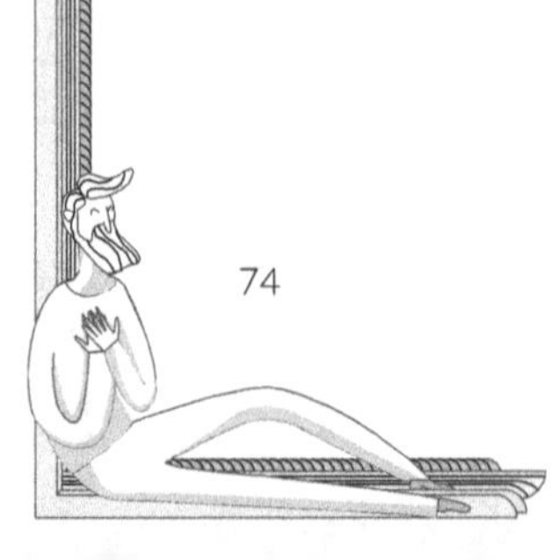

Nilda Chiaraviglio

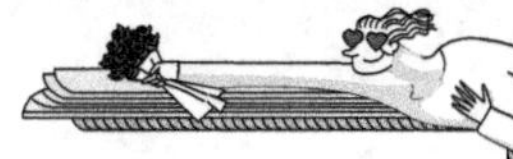

Fill out the following table individually:

	Expectations in the relationship		Individual needs		Problems that arose
	Achieved	Not achieved	Achieved	Not achieved	
Explicit	1.	1.	1.	1.	1.
	2.	2.	2.	2.	2.
	3.	3.	3.	3.	3.
	…	…	…	…	…
Implied	1.	1.	1.	1.	1.
	2.	2.	2.	2.	2.
	3.	3.	3.	3.	3.
	…	…	…	…	…

Some additional questions can help with self-knowledge and reveal information about the type of affective bond that the couple has:

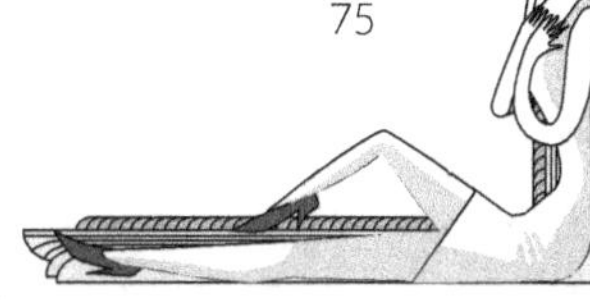

🐾   *Every time you think differently about a topic, do you each believe that your reason is unique and true?*

🐾   *When your partner expresses an interest, desire or personal taste, do you assume it as a personal challenge? Do you neglect it because it is not your business? Or do you ask him if he needs you to collaborate with something?*

🐾   *Do you think you know what your partner's expectations are about building this relationship? Do you imagine them, or do you ask them to really find out?*

🐾   *Is there always someone who makes all the decisions, or do you make them by areas? Is there always one who dominates and the other who submits? Is this comfortable for both?*

🐾   *Do you consider you have built a reciprocal relationship? Do either of you feel overloaded or overwhelmed?*

🐾   *Have you felt injustice, inadequacy, or helplessness in some areas of the relationship?*

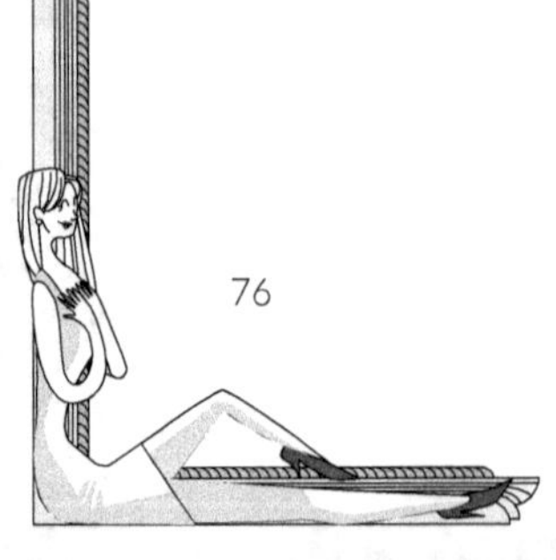

Nilda Chiaraviglio

> *It is a good time to "put the cards on the table" talking about feelings, individual needs, ways of communicating and renewing agreements based on an open dialogue, listening to each other with great **curiosity**, that is, without judgments, prejudices, interpretations and, therefore, without defending oneself from the opinions of the other.*

Conversation spaces

Proposing activities is usually useful for people to reflect on the different roles they play as partners, spouses or parents. It is common for some couples to play all the roles *mixed together* and do not distinguish when they carry out activities as a couple or parent, nor do they create different spaces and conversations for each of those roles.

The following chart is useful for reflecting on the preferences of both partners regarding the different areas and roles they play, which ones they would like to modify, and which ones they want to keep.

Each line of the exercise involves a reflection on the preferences of each member of the couple on each of the topics. The list may change according to each case.

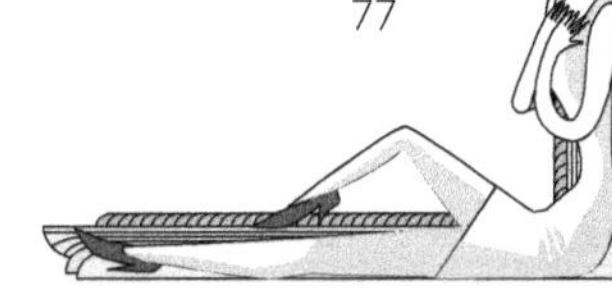

Topics	Initial contract	Deviation	Current contract
Time (hours we want to share)			
Space (meters of distance between the two)			
Individual life priorities			
Trust and communication			
Individual core values			
Sexual relationship and faithfulness			
Money, expenses and administration			
Roles, shareable and non-shareable			
Likes in amusements and free time			

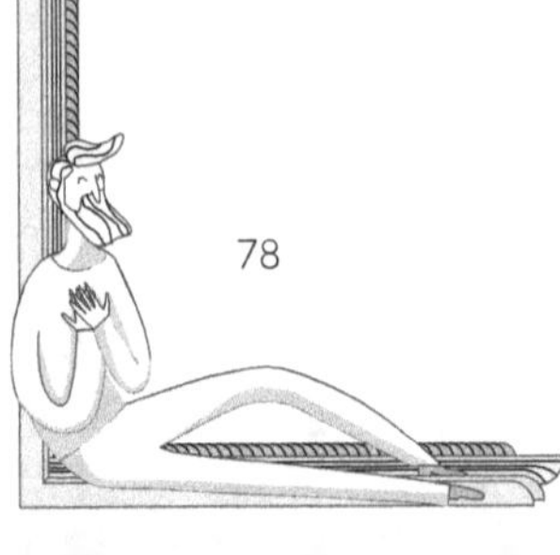

Nilda Chiaraviglio

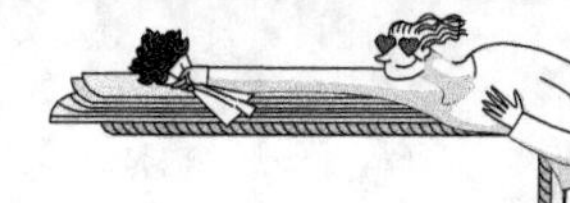

What was and is the couple's contract desired for each of the members of the couple? It may happen that they discover that the model desired by one of them has little to do with that of the other. When there are children, it is possible to modify the contract for another of only parents or parenting partners.

&   When both parties take charge of their problems, what they like and dislike, they free the other from the burden of an impossible quest: «You must make me happy.»

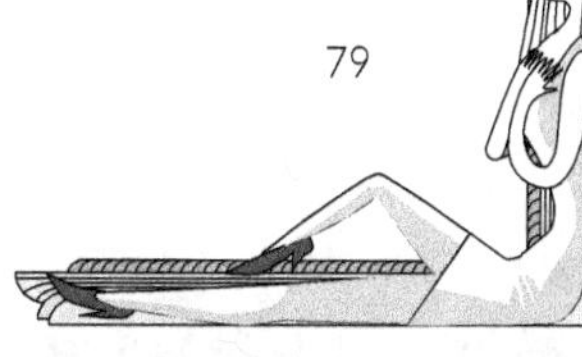

05

Emotions and love

Self-knowledge gives us the power to name emotions accurately, it warns us if our belief system is in line with reality or not.

If we are walking distracted and bump into a person who gets angry and insults us, we can interpret the situation in two very different ways:

- *We could get angry too and defend ourselves in our own way.*

- *Feel a little compassion and keep walking calmly.*

Our emotions depend on how we interpret what happens, and that interpretation depends on our life history and how we want to think and live.

Misunderstandings

Let me propose an exercise to become aware of how much we can make mistakes when we interpret what our partner does, thinks or feels.

Part One

At the end of each day, have **Member 1** of the couple fill out the following table:

My partner's behavior	How I interpret each behavior
1.	1.
2.	2.
3.	3.

At the end, **Member 2** can already classify the interpretations into three categories:

- **Very successful:** *that was in fact my intention.*

- **Somewhat successful:** *fair success.*

- **Far removed:** *that had NOTHING to do with my intention.ciones.*

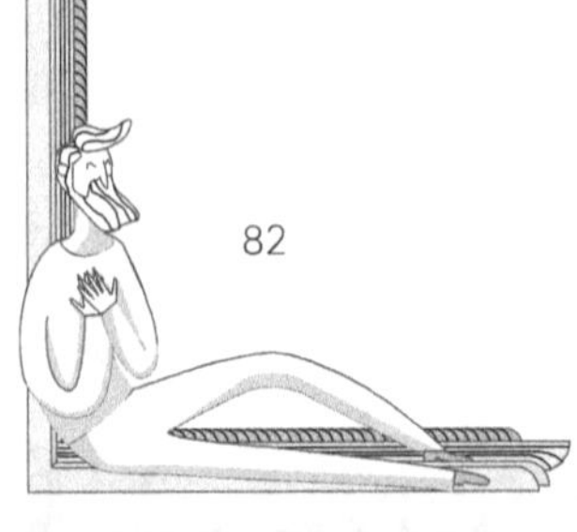

Nilda Chiaraviglio

They shouldn't talk about anything yet.

Part Two

At the end of each day, have **Member 2** of the couple fill out the following table:

Times of the day when I felt like... (choose a behavior)	What was happening just before I felt that urge?
1.	1.
2.	2.
3.	3.

At the end, **Member 1** can already classify the interpretations into three categories:

- **Very successful:** *my partner fully realized what was going to happen.*

- **Somewhat successful:** *when he sensed it, he didn't give it importance.*

- **Far removed:** *he had no idea.*

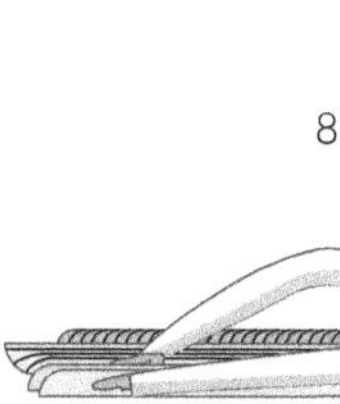

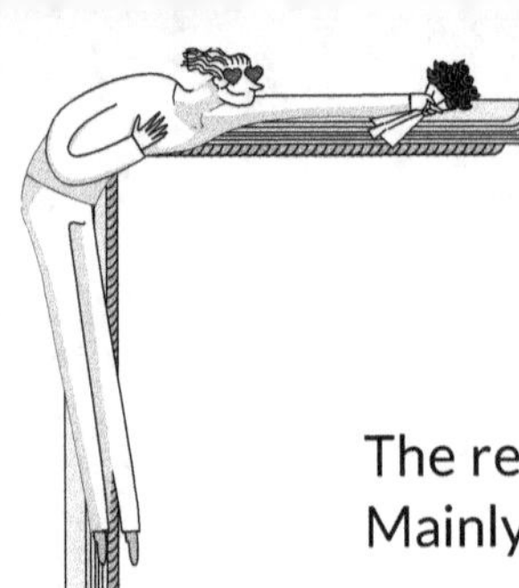

The result of this exercise is usually of two types Mainly:

- *Refreshing for the bond, and the partners begin to realize how they are functioning.*

- *They use it to sharpen their fights; they will argue whenever the other is wrong about the interpretations.*

Either way, it's good information to transform what they deem appropriate.

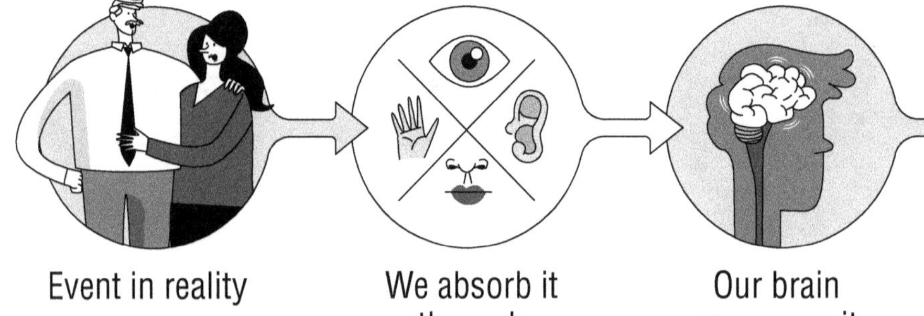

Nilda Chiaraviglio

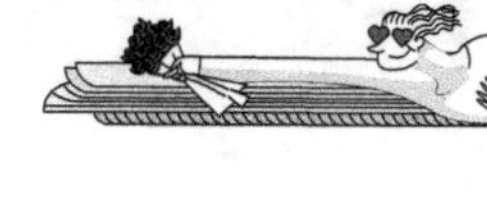

Where do emotions come from?

& «All pain comes from a wrong thought».

The previous sentence was said by Neale Donald Walsch, and I think it is extremely useful, because it reminds us of how we produce our emotions; it is possible that they empower us and we decide to pay attention to the thoughts that make us feel pain and transform them.

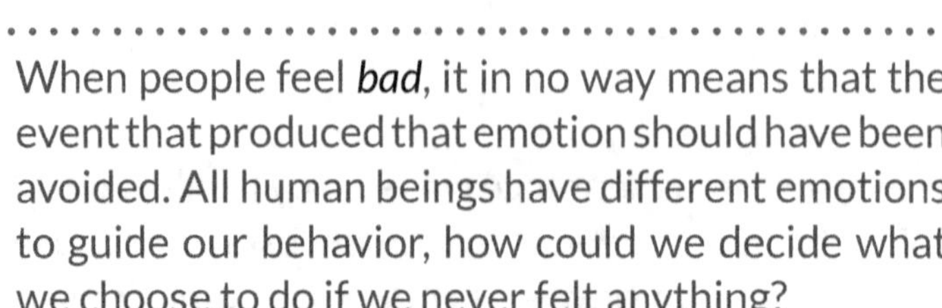

> When people feel *bad*, it in no way means that the event that produced that emotion should have been avoided. All human beings have different emotions to guide our behavior, how could we decide what we choose to do if we never felt anything?

Our emotions and feelings are like the email that the unconscious uses to inform us about the belief system with which we decipher reality.

&   What *bothers* us is that interpretation, never the facts themselves.

Emotions under prejudice

In our culture, some emotions have had a bad reputation, such as anger, rage, sadness, melancholy, rejection, confusion, insecurity, among many others; however, they all have a **positive intention behind**.

Contradictions, doubts and mistakes motivate our desire to improve. Why modify something that is fine? It is what is wrong that allows us to evolve.

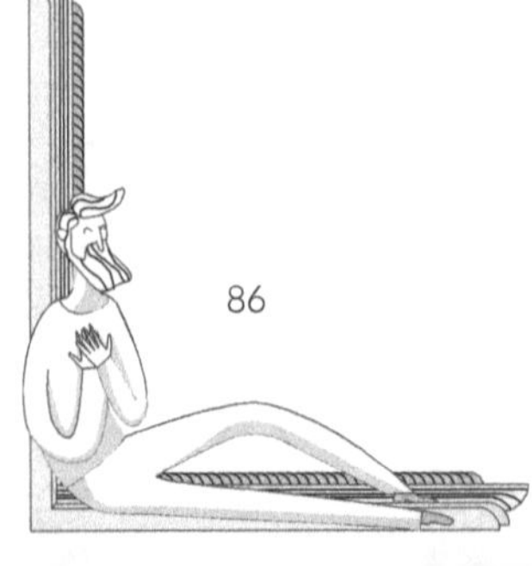

Nilda Chiaraviglio

Throughout life, we learn that:

- *It's not so bad to be wrong*

- *Nor is it so good to be well.*

- *It's not so necessary to be needed.*

- *Nor is it so important to be important.*

If we learn to use our discomforts as a source of inspiration to optimize our quality of life, we will manage life according to our desire. Any event, no matter how painful or unpleasant it may be, can be transformed into growth through a process of alchemy, mixing reflection and appropriate techniques.

Emotional catalog

It is important to expand the range of emotions that we allow ourselves to experience, as they are our internal information system. They are **ours** and we can do with them as we please.

When we ignore, reject or deny them, we go against our **self-knowledge** and stop learning from the information they bring us, which increases the possibility of making mistakes.

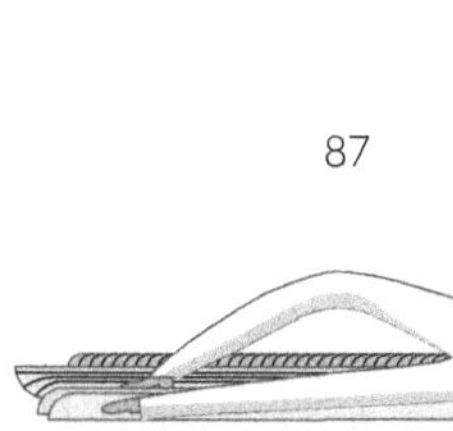

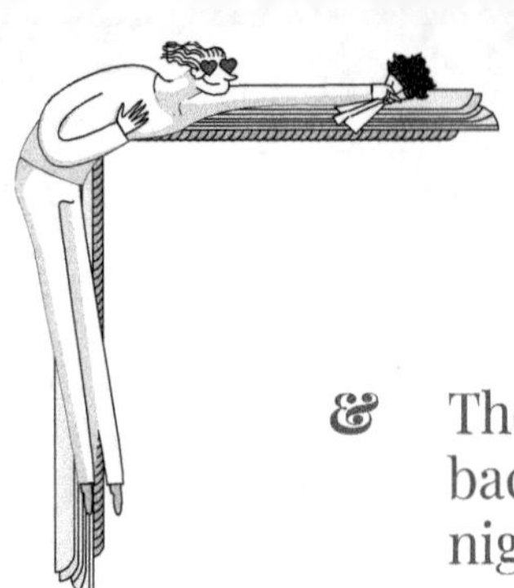

The emotions you reject will come back to you like a ghost on a stormy night.

    Did you pay attention to how you interpret what's going on around you?

    What kind of judgments and prejudices do you use when looking at other people's behavior?

    How many times a day do you make interpretations of what is happening?

    Do you do it consciously or does it just **happen to you?**

    Does your partner know what your system of interpretations is?

    Do you know that an interpretation is an invention which is only yours?

    Have you ever tried to find more than one interpretation for the same event?

    How many times have you thought that your partner misunderstood you?

    How do you feel about that?

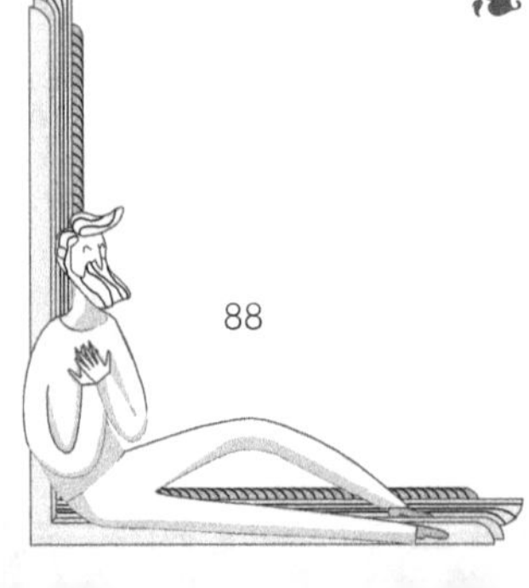

Nilda Chiaraviglio

The myth of forgiveness

When we feel attacked, it is common to hear advice such as «Forget it, it is better to forgive», or things like that. In reality, it is impossible for this to happen just like that, and even more so if it was something very important. No one forgets significant pain, it's not that easy.

> True forgiveness is opening a process, an inner work in which the origin of pain is discovered in order to turn it into a personal teaching, in **self-knowledge**, and in the development of skills and resources. This way, we will continue to remember the experience, but without any regrets or sorrow, and even with gratitude.

Virtues and habits

Emotions awaken skills and abilities in us, for example, if as children we are exposed to an environment of great competition and little transparency, discomfort will make us learn to be strong; this will constitute a resource for success in the future.

What would you drive a nail with? There is prob-ably nothing better than a hammer; however, what if you tried to comb or style your hair with one?

&   Each skill is useful for whatever it's useful; it is up to us what we decide to use it for.

For better or for worse

The same thing happens with the skills we develop from our emotions: they are good and useful for what they are, and if we want to use them to solve any other problem, it is very likely that they will be inefficient.

Virtue and self-destructive habit (using a hammer to comb your hair) can represent the same emotion and behavior in different circumstances. What is the line that transforms a skill into a destructive habit? The answer lies in the following reflection:

&   Is what I'm going to do useful for me? Does it lead me to achieve what I want?

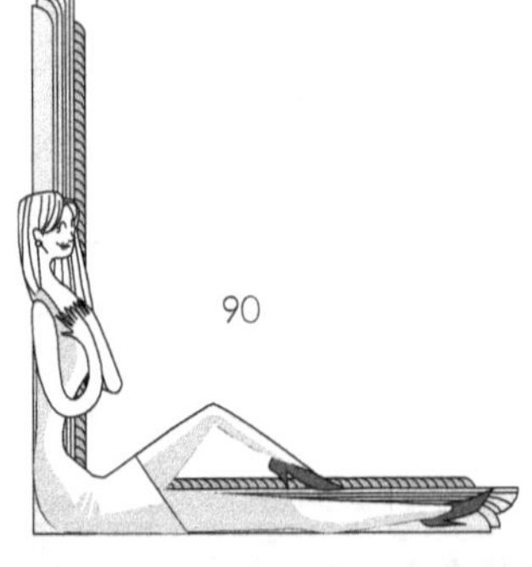

Nilda Chiaraviglio

If you are not aware of what your main emotional skills are, nor do you know when they lead you towards destructive habit or virtue, I propose that you perform the following exercise:

My skills are:	They are useful for:	They bring me trouble when:	What new skills would I use if the old ones don't work?
1.	1.	1.	1.
2.	2.	2.	2.
3.	3.	3.	3.
4.	4.	4.	4.
5.	5.	5.	5.

Highways and roads

A behavioral habit is a road that we have repeated many times and that has already become a highway in our brain: it is new, it has five lanes, it is fast and well paved.

& There are unconscious behaviors that are no longer efficient in responding to new problems, needs or interests.

For example, when we learn to drive a car, it is necessary to coordinate many activities involving eyes, hands and feet; at first it is very complex, but, with practice, we manage to coordinate them all with relative ease: **a little path was built.**

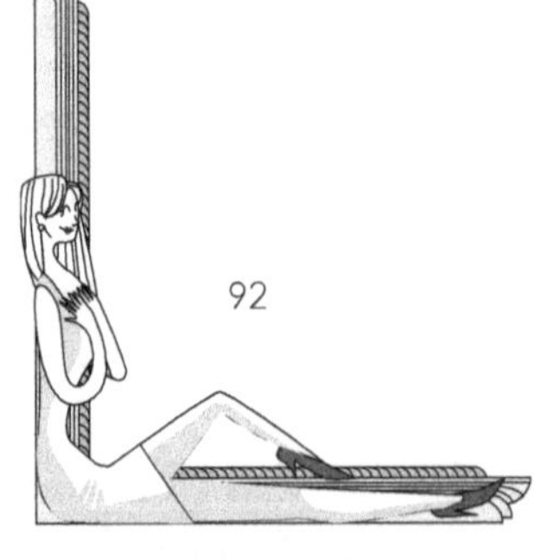

Nilda Chiaraviglio

With a little more practice, we do all that together at the same time, plus listening to music and chatting with our travel companion: **it has already become a highway**, a habit or behavior determined by the unconscious.

When we realize that the results of our behavior are unpleasant or uncomfortable for us, it is time to ask our brain to create a new path with aspirations to also become a highway.

Some of the questions that help the possibility of expanding our consciousness are:

- *When was the last time a behavior or habit worked for you in your relationship?*

- *Which of the two members of the couple enjoys frustration the most, we're talking about the frustration arised from an unwanted result, caused by the usual behavior?*

- *Who would be the first to recognize and admit that the outcome of the decision they made caused an upset just because they did more of the same?*

- *Which of the two needs the situation to always remain the same or worse?*

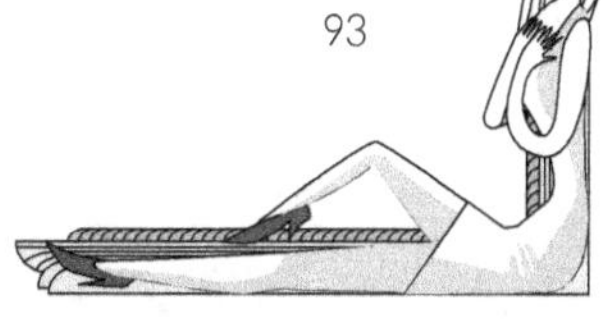

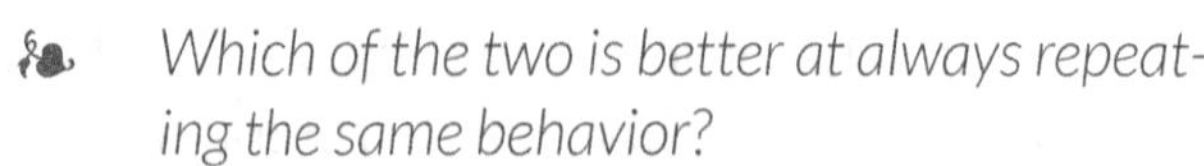

Which of the two is better at always repeating the same behavior?

& If a different way of getting along was implemented, would the relationship end?

From within

In another part of the book we already wrote down a list of what we like and dislike about our partner; now we can utilize it to build a point of view from within. Let's start by asking ourselves: what is the use of sharing my life with this person?

For any conversation that is aimed at solving problems, it is advisable to establish what we have called «Internal Position».

It is very exhausting that the entire relationship is put at stake whenever we talk about a problem. In those cases, it is common to hear phrases such as: «This doesn´t make any sense anymore», «Go away, I just want to be at peace», «I do not know what you are with me for», etc.

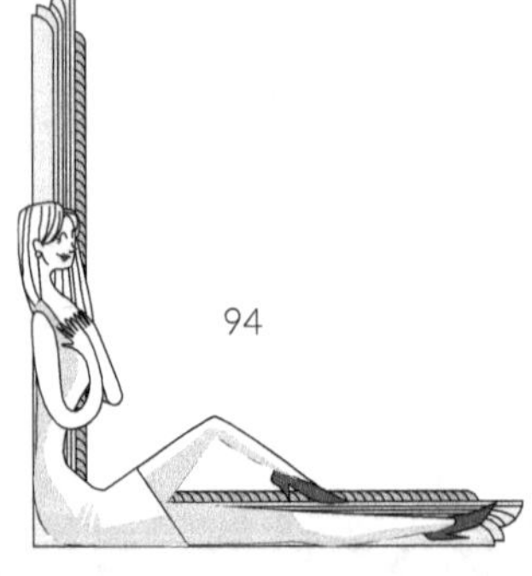

Nilda Chiaraviglio

What I like:	How does that improve my life?
1.	1.
2.	2.
3.	3.
4.	4.
5.	5.

People threaten their partners with leaving the relationship and walking away in a rage. These practices damage trust and also the bond.

& If those behaviors continue, sooner or later they both will end up separating.

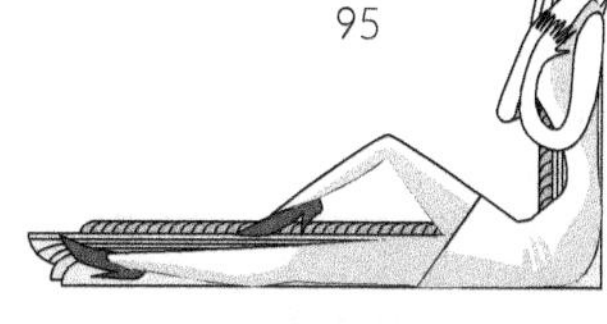

Things are meant to be talked about

Building a relationship without talking and without **self-knowledge** is almost impossible, mainly for two reasons:

- *Decisionsrest in the hands of the speaker, and therefore what he says will sometimes-match the tastes of the other and other times the other will disagree.*

- *Whoever makes the **decision** makes up and also interprets what the other likes and why they do things.*

& We have to talk about the problems and also about the pleasant things. Remember that «the truth will set us free».

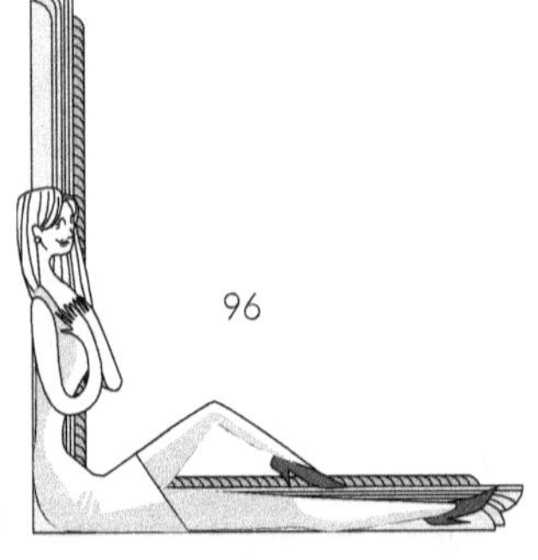

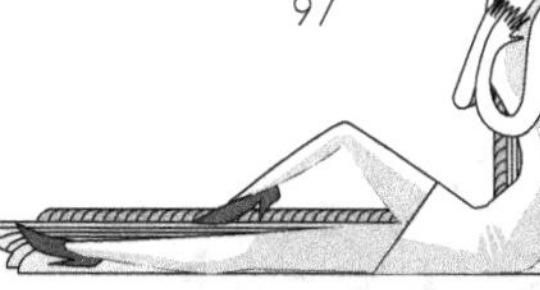

06

The great dilemma: choosing a partner

Most of us human beings have *suffered for love*. How to choose a partner is perhaps the most sought-after secret on this planet, because we could discover the secret of eternal life, but spending it alone seems like an unpleasant option. We may find a way to make millions of dollars; however, who are we going to share them with?

At First Sight

Why one specific person and not another? The conflicts observed in the couple retain an imprint that often has its origin in unconscious commitments that led the two involved to prefer each other over anyone else.

In general, when couples narrate their first meeting, they tell us the updated version of the past, each member from their point of view. They have little or no idea of what attracted them to each other, beyond matters of chance.

Each one unknowingly protects
themselves from something by
choosing a specific person.

The adult is defined by the sociocultural context
in which they have spent their childhood, both by
socioeconomic and geographical conditions, and
by the type of family in which they grew up. All this
determines a selection.

Nilda Chiaraviglio

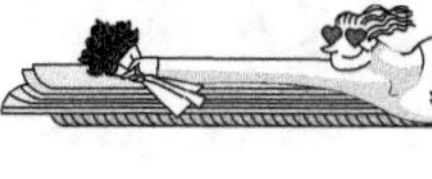

20 things about my mother

The process of choosing the partner can go through the following stages:

1. *In all human beings, an **imaginary behavior** linked to the process of separation is activated, especially from the mother (or the person who raised us).*

2. *The relationship with the couple is the closest affective bond we have after that of our mother.*

3. *When we feel attracted to a person, we remember childhood experiences to find a good **mother** to take care of us.*

4. *In our imagination, there is a **totally** good mother, and in the rest of the world there is all the **bad**, **threatening** and **persecuting**.*

5. *Thanks to the imagination, we separate the **good** and **bad** parts of the mother.*

6. *When we choose a partner, it is almost impossible for us to dissociate that relationship from the ones we wait for with nostalgia.*

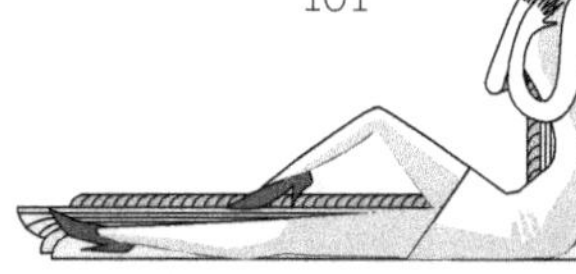

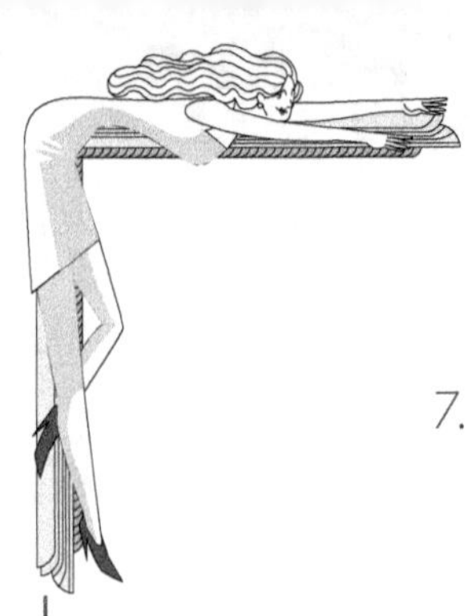

7. *From the unconscious, we expect the couple to make up for all the affective deficiencies we had in childhood.*

8. *It is very difficult for immature people to endure the processes described here without feeling very bad.*

9. *If that inner reality continues to be rejected, it could become pathological.*

10. *When we have an inability to accept that there are **good** and **bad** parts in the same person —taking our mother as a reference— we develop a total rejection of any and all relationships.*

11. *During falling in love, infantile processes develop that lead to .«all or nothing» or .«bad or good», with few middle points.*

12. *Maturity is equivalent to accepting that our mother was never and never will be everything we needed or wanted.*

13. *Adulthood begins (we stop being children) so that we can embark on a long-term loving-erotic relationship.*

14. *Recognition of the imperfection in our*

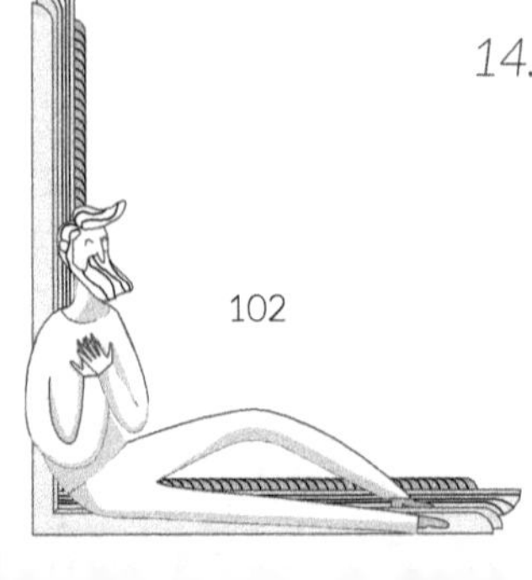

Nilda Chiaraviglio

partner and in ourselves, acceptance that hostile feelings are born within the bond, however good it may be.

15. *If the satisfactory part is **sufficient**, we can absolutely disagree with the other party without rejecting them. We will be able to understand and comprehend them without having to share their point of view, emotions or behaviors.*

16. *If the satisfactory part is **insufficient**, we will limit love relationships, since extending them would mean running the risk of losing the idealized image of them being enough to meet our demands.*

17. *Those who have never managed to establish **healthy** relationships may become depressed or repeat the cycle.*

18. *When we use fantasy to generate expectations that something or someone will come to satisfy all our needs, the **object** of this idealization will inevitably crash into reality.*

19. *Almost all love bonds have a way of idealizing the partner; this optimism overrides anxiety and programs frustration.*

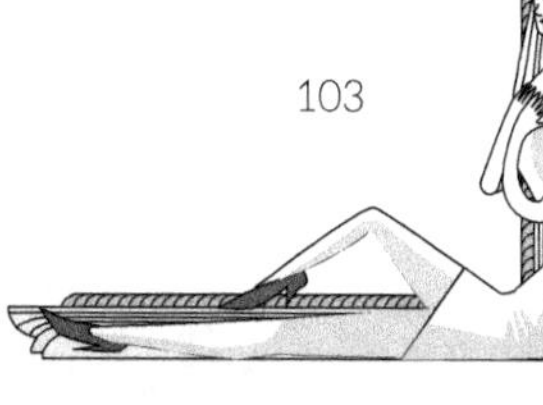

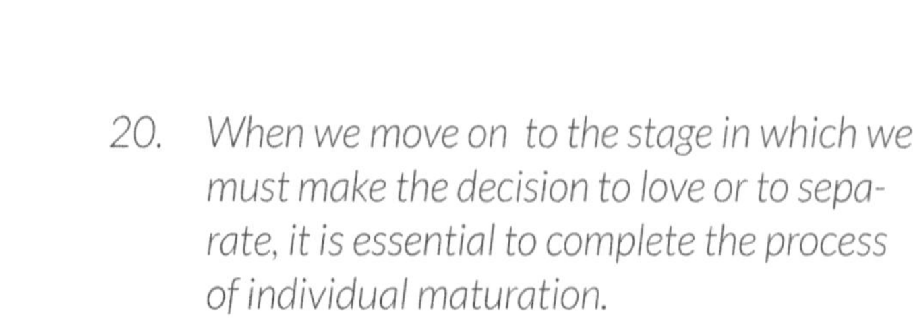

My fantasy

The inability to maintain the idealization of the partner can manifest itself through behaviors such as becoming adventurous, cold, liar, critical, dissatisfied, political, polygamous, insecure, victim or even self-defined as a savior.

Most likely, one will choos a partner who is similar to one's mother or father (or exactly the opposite), and turns out to be a model of security, comfort and well-being. Research reports that these are the ones that get destabilized the fastest.

New models

It seems that the more innovative the couple models are, the greater the chances of success. Internet, apps, social networks and technology show us testimonies of couples of different races, cultures, religions, ages, languages, etc., who are consolidated in very original ways and, apparently, tailored to measure.

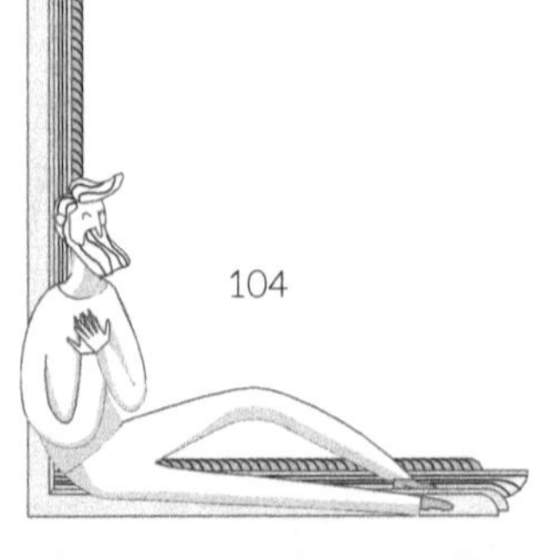

Nilda Chiaraviglio

At first glance —and even more so after the pandemic— values linked to security, safety, community, land, parenthood or the conventional family have lost a bit of appeal today, and people appear to be more attracted by differences, the possibility of knowing other worlds, relationships with shorter and more intense deadlines, international travel or permission to have multiple relationships.

These phenomena make us reflect on the theory of choosing the partner of the future. We can ask ourselves some questions to remember how we chose our partner and how they changed:

- *What was it like when you met? Place, clothing, context, (photo).*

- *How were you feeling before?*

- *How old were you both?*

- *Who acted first? How did the other respond?*

- *Why was there such an attraction?*

- *Did anything displease you?*

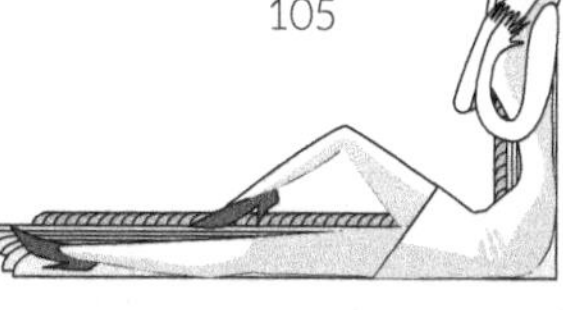

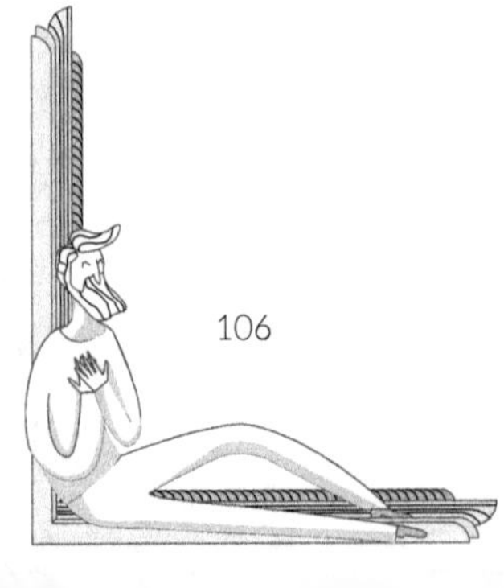

- What did you think or imagine about each other?

- Was it a new feeling or had you felt it before?

- What did your friends and family think?

- First fight.

- What did you do to feel loved?

- What were you talking about?

- What did you stop doing that you used to do before?

- Who paid the bills?

- Was there jealousy?

- Were there explicit and implicit controls, rules, conditions, or obligations?

- What were the biggest changes?

Nilda Chiaraviglio

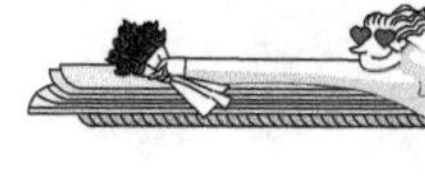

Thick Filters

We all have pretty strong preferences about what we would never choose in a partner. Do you know your own thick filters? We usually establish them by areas:

- *Physically.*

- *Intellectually.*

- *In how my partner acts when he/she is in a relationship (jealous, loud, violent, submissive, etc.).*

- *Because of their social status, religion, economic level, etc.*

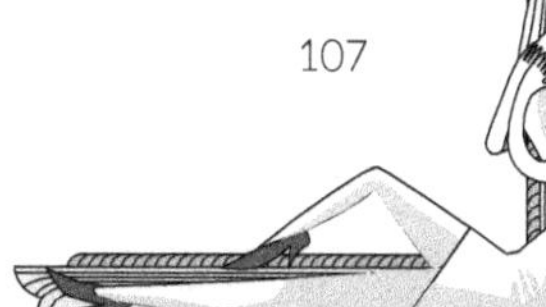

My filters

I invite you to make three different lists answering the following questions:

 *1. What would **you never** allow a partner again?*

*2. What would **you never** do again in a relationship?*

3. How did I manage to hurt myself in relationships?

I will never allow...	I will never...	How do I get hurt?
1.	1.	1.
2.	2.	2.
3.	3.	3.
...	...	...

The behaviors that are repeated in the three lists are the common denominators. They are the commitment to yourself that you will never again waste time with someone who has any of the characteristics of those foolish factors.

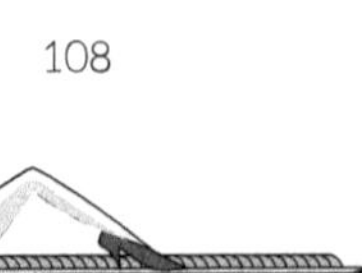

Nilda Chiaraviglio

There are other questions that will help you let go of the past:

    What do you miss from your past? What I long for becomes empowerment

    What are the three main pains of what you have already experienced? What hurts becomes wisdom.

The affective bond achieved by two adults is the responsibility of each one at 50%:

    What did you do, feel or think to achieve the result you have today in life?

    What are the consequences of your behaviors? Behaviors have consequences.

    Which of your behaviors would you modify to transform your consequences?

& As we can see, freedom of choice is actually much smaller than people think.

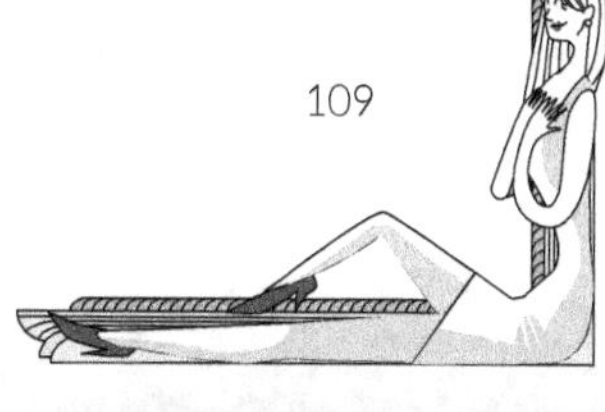

07

Different types of couples

How can we try to understand the mysteries of the world? Impossible. The more we learn, the more we realize how much we ignore.In the same way, classifying the types of couples implies reducing a universe of differences and specificities to a few common characteristics.

> & Every couple who decides to build a bond thinks that they both have the same concept of a couple.

The common elements are commitment and eroticism, which with attitudes, disposition, care, attention, knowledge, respect and responsibility form a solid structure.

Couples according to their constitution

Couples are forged with the circumstances of their members and with the context that surrounds them: families, social environment, institutions, whether or not they think about forming a family. There are some common characteristics in couples:

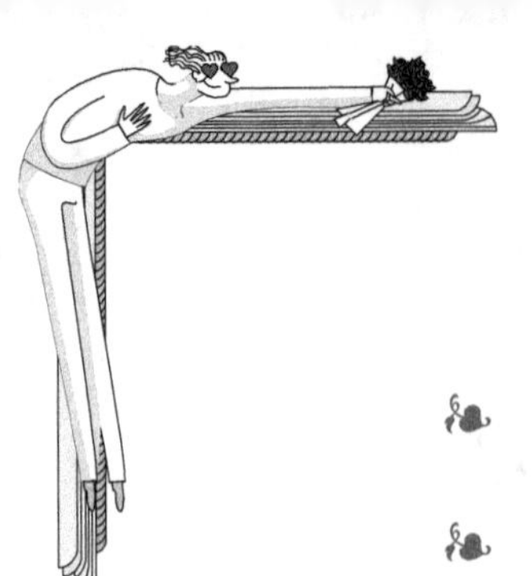

> 🐾   *Their dynamics.*
>
> 🐾   *Diversity.*
>
> 🐾   *Context.*
>
> 🐾   *Construction of the erotic space.*

&   There are no pure forms of couples, there are only some marked characteristics.

Romantic couple

They were also called «couples of the night», in the NINETEENTH century. Its members think that they are immersed in a revolutionary act, that they determine a different order of things and a rupture with the world. Falling in love melts them and isolates them from everything; its main features are:

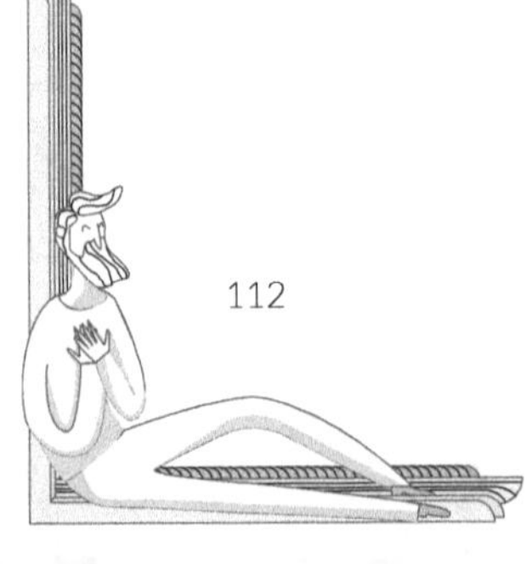

Nilda Chiaraviglio

- *They make their own rules and break those of their families of origin.*

- *They create fantasies that validate each other.*

- *Infatuation is different from romanticism.*

- *The bond is the most important thing.*

- *The idea of children is **not** important, it depends on the cycle of the couple.*

- *Eroticism is intense and unique, involving all parts of the body, which is a source of desire and renewed discovery.*

It has three stages of evolution:

- **Egg of two yolks:** *fusion and projection of the good and the bad of each one within its unique and magical space; two yolks linked by a single egg white (the link). It usually occurs in young couples who «fall in love with love itself».*

- **Why do I want to leave?:** *Since nothing can remain identical to itself, feelings of uneasiness begin to appear, both of them drown inside the egg, and the need for individual spaces begins to appear. Felling imperceptibly begin to appear, like anger, frustrations, aggression, guilt, distrust and sadness. The failure of revolution. Who is to blame? It seems like infidelities —not necessarily from a lover—, it can be a book, friends, children, work, sleep, etc. Betrayals of the original contract that read: «You will always be the most important thing in my life, and since I can't get angry, I get sad».*

- **Fusion versus separation:** *fusion and separation are just moments, so the task is to regulate the distance. This entails a difficulty, because it is experienced as a betrayal or threat to the original agreements, even if at this point the merge feels like suffocation.*

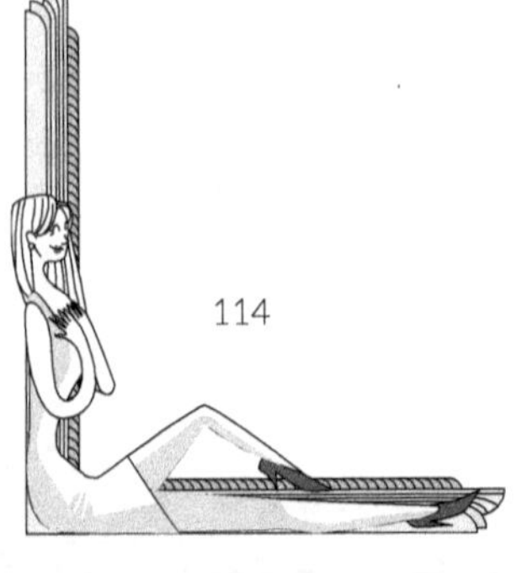

Nilda Chiaraviglio

Arranged couple

It is in which different people intervene in the opin-
ion of the members: families of origin, institutions,
contexts:

- *Its purpose is to form a family like ours.*

- *It is an agreement where the roles are estab-
  lished in harmony.*

- *They function more as parents than as
  a couple. Having children is expected; it
  means success.*

- *The families (of the two) confirm the identity.*

- *Continuity is very important.*

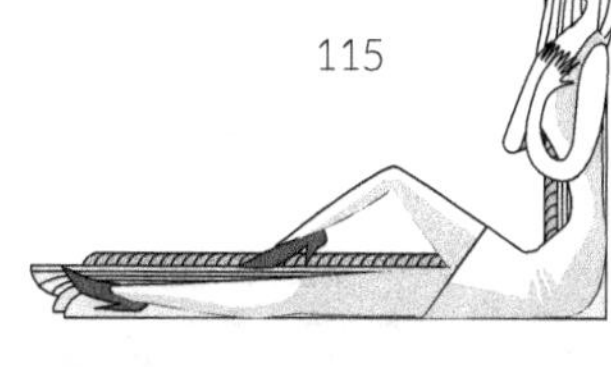

Kangaroo couple

It occurs especially in adolescence, when they come together after a good time of dating or courtship. Difficulties come when, after being married for a while, they are bored and without a future. In their inner world they are inseparable and, from the comfortable kangaroo bag, observe and interact with the world. Its main features are:

- *The important thing is to belong.*

- *They stick to their children and stop growing; there is parental deficit because they all look like siblings.*

- *Collusion: they come together to satisfy needs not covered by each other's parents.*

- *They love each other long after the separation.*

- *They are a similar otherness.*

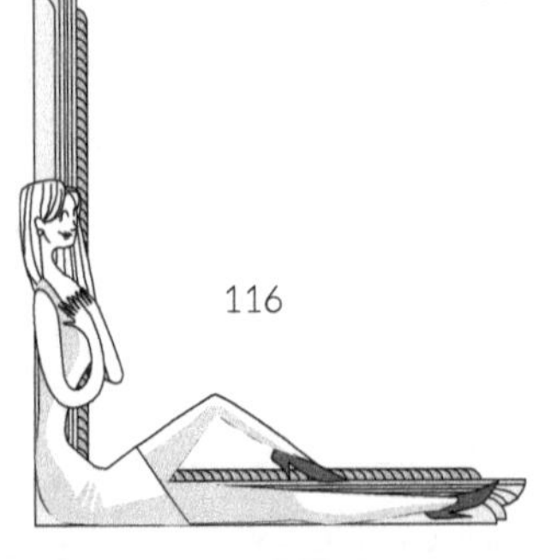

Nilda Chiaraviglio

- *They grow together, although they are autonomous.*

- *There is never any fusion, nor confusion.*

- *The fraternal zone is very important.*

- *What nourishes them is the bond.*

- *The separations (all of them) generate transformations in the bond, there is always disorganization of the external and internal world.*

- *Parenthood is a disgrace in that period.*

> The crisis comes because a different sexuality is sought, because of the need to individualize, because of growth lag, because of the choice of different paths or because of the invasion or conflicts of interest with the families of origin.

Extended friendship couple

This type of relationship begins to take an increasingly widespread presence in Western society, especially in urban areas, towards the end of the NINETEENTH and early TWENTIETH centuries. Among the most outstanding features we can find:

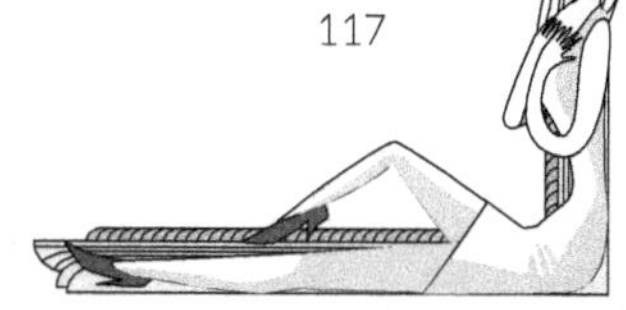

- *They have mutual friends.*

- *They get along well: they are kind to each other.*

- *They build the bond without the need for falling in love.*

- *They both have had other partners.*

- *They both enjoy a high degree of autonomy.*

- *They learned to be very careful with idealization.*

- *They are medium or fully grown adults, with children older than teenagers. If they decide have another child, there is a renegotiation of the dependencies.*

- *Sexuality is very pleasant, low passion in the emotional.*

- *Broad communication, dialogue, negotiation.*

- *Mostly shared desires, interests and values.*

- *They usually live separately, that is, each in their own home.*

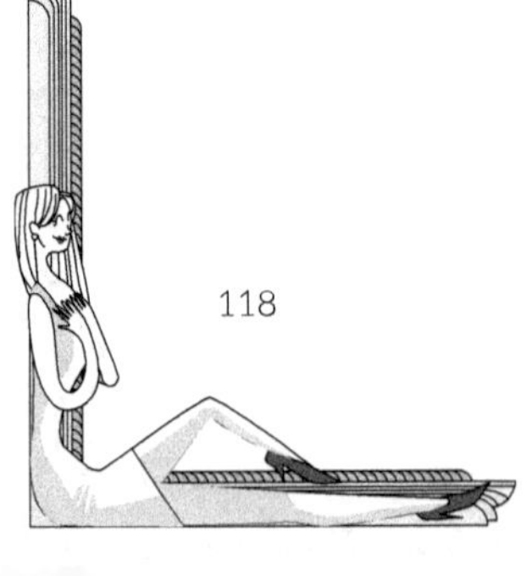

Nilda Chiaraviglio

> Difficulties arise when one of them gets sick, or due to work and money problems, or because of death or terminal illnesses of the parents. The readjustments in this type of bond are quite fast; discomforts and supports are simply discussed.

Forced couple

They are made in most migrations (home, neighborhood, social status, etc.). Any relationship is complex, but if a move is forced, some aspects become important to watch. Its characteristics are:

There was already a couple before the migration.

Something happens that forces movement.

A massive and ambiguous loss appears, mourning, hatred, conflict of loyalties, fear, curiosity and anxiety that causes nostalgia, sadness, change, uncertainty.

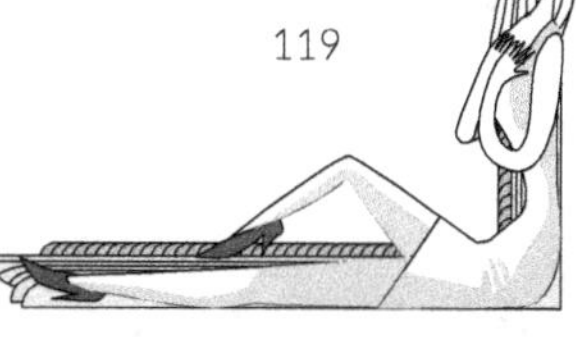

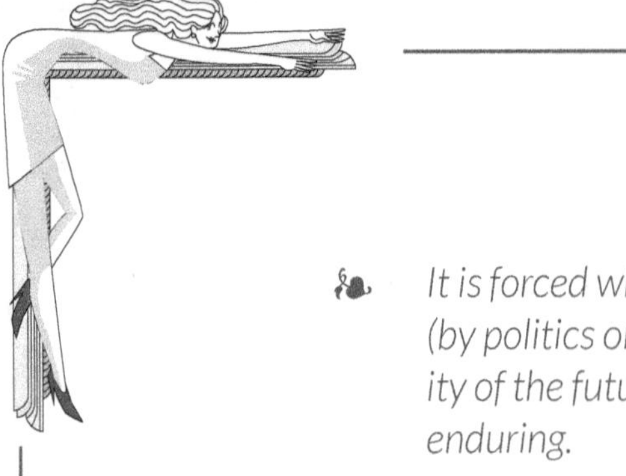

It is forced when it comes to «life or death» (by politics or economics). The unpredictability of the future is presented, surviving and enduring.

All links (hierarchies, roles, economic position, belonging) are disrupted.

Children are a nucleus of anguish.

> The overload of conflicts and difficulties distance them from their tasks as a couple, make them sick, or turn them into just parents; there is a loss of limits, which leads to lack of intimacy and aggression due to the desire to flee. It is necessary to determine what the needs and aspirations of each one are.

Couples according to their relationship

This classification is based on how the members of the couple interact and provide other reflections on the individual and their affective relationship in the middle of a crisis stage. All can be stable or fragile.

> All these reflections can be useful when a relationship enters a stage of crisis or conflict, to renew all agreements.

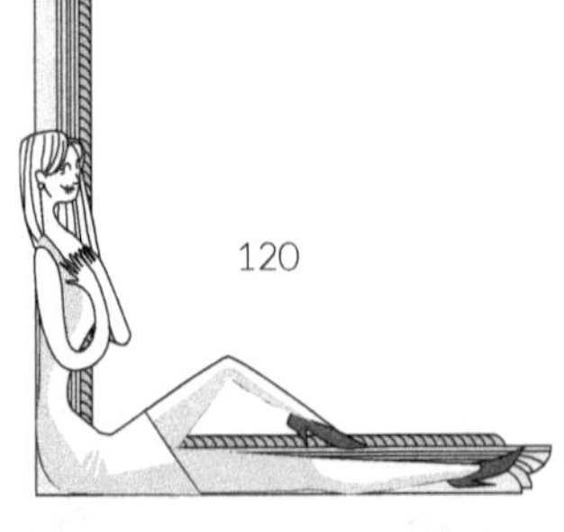

Nilda Chiaraviglio

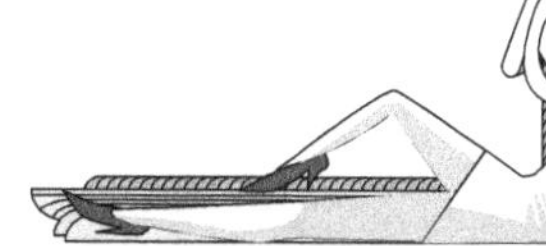

Type of relationship	Characteristics
Asymmetric relationship	Each member has roles, activities that complement the other: man-woman, active-passive, knows-learns, etc. The goal is long-term.
Coordinated relationship	Each one knows themself and finds a way to share their life and adapt to the other. Interchangeable roles. They are open to the outside.
Formal relationship	Each one's script is established by the family or society: knight-princess. The form and aesthetics of the relationship are more important than the people or the relationship.
Object relationship	Each serves the purposes of the other. Here marriage of convenience fits. The goal is to achieve social or economic ends. People or relationship are an instrument.

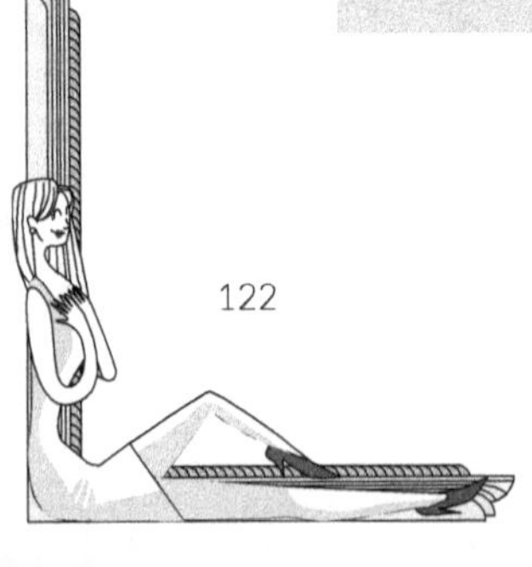

Nilda Chiaraviglio

Advantages	Disadvantages
It allows the compensation of the shortcomings an emotional deficiencies of its members.	They end up in a deadly routine.
Openness to the possibilities of originality.	They reach heartbreak.
Develops a sense of security.	They are impoverishing or rigid.
It allows you to escape from an unpleasant situation.	They can reach violence.

08

What does it depend on?

&   The codependent is an unconscious
     ally of the problems of their relative
     or close person.

«Dependency» and «codependency» are two related
terms, but we must be able to differentiate them.

   When we talk about **bond dependency**, we are
faced with a case in which one of the parties that
make up the relationship feels that they *need* the
other to be able to live, and comes to deeply fear a
rupture or breakup.

&   Dependent people are generally
     insecure, irresponsible for their own
     well-being, and develop excessive
     and pathological attachment.

On the other hand, emotional **codependency** implies one person's addiction to another's dependency; that is, in a relationship, one of the parties can develop an obsession with the other person, believing them to be essential for their life and needing them all the time (emotional dependence), while, the other party, can become addicted to seeking to help their partner unconditionally and also fosteringtheir good and wellbeing (codependency).

> Bonds of emotional dependency and codependency do not necessarily need to develop in loving relationships; it is also possible for them to occur between friends and family. The important thing is to keep in mind that the codependent feeds the dependence of another person, feeling the urge to collaborate with them and avoid all kinds of evil.

&	Who is codependent is being a collaborator, probably without realizing it, to make the situation worse, helping the dependent to remain in their comfort zone.

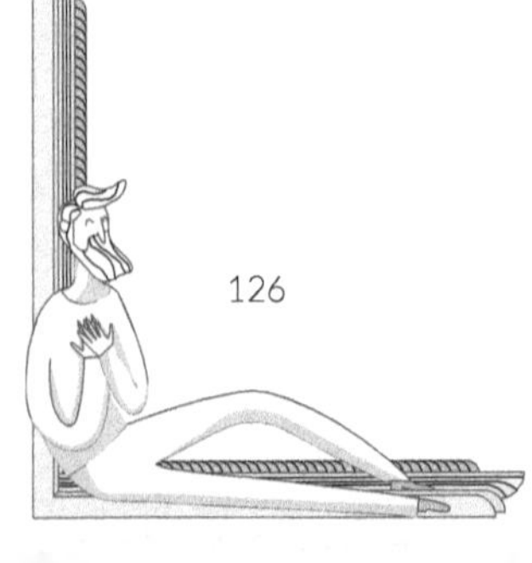

 Nilda Chiaraviglio

Codependents without "pending"

It is necessary to know that, for there to be codependency, it is not mandatory that there be someone dependent. Codependents are experts in satisfying other's needs, leaving aside their own.

They help a loved one no matter when, where or how, because for them that is the priority. The same applies to emotional dependency: if someone is emotionally dependent on another person, that does not mean that the person they depend on is codependent.

How to know?

How can we identify codependency to avoid fulfilling that role or even depending on someone who exercises it over us?

Have you ever wondered why codependency occurs?

While there is no recipe for what should happen in a person's life for them to become *dependent*, some upbringing circumstances can lead to the development of such personalities.

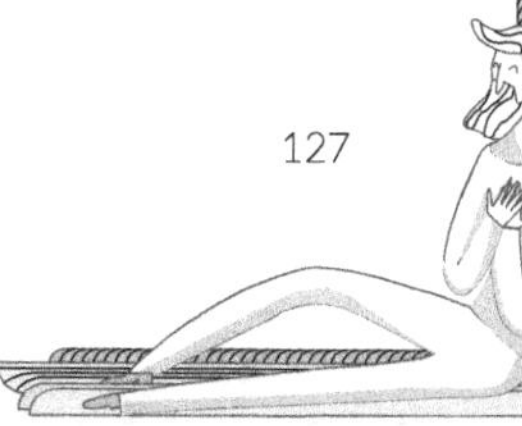

Children who grow up in these solitary environments have difficulty understanding that their own needs are important and must be met, because no one taught them in time. They took the role of assisting their caregivers without considering that they themselves were also worthy of attention and care. So why would this change as we grow up?

Keep an eye out

Identify emotional codependency:

- *Are you a person who gives up everything to provide help to others?*

- *Are you someone who feels constantly insecure about losing their bonds?*

- *Are the people you interact with like that?*

- *Do you find it difficult to recognize your needs and desires?*

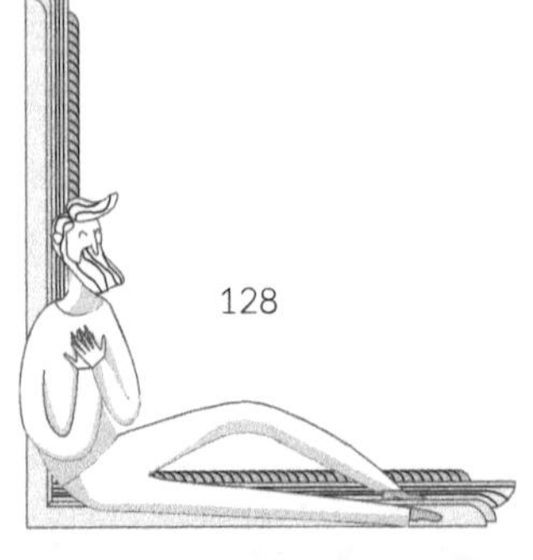

Nilda Chiaraviglio

Codependent people:

- *Always put others first.*

- *Leave themselves at the bottom of the list.*

- *Feel responsible for the feelings of others.*

- *Are emotionally responsible to a fault.*

- *Think a lot about how people feel about what they do or don't do.*

- *For them it is terrible to hurt others.*

- *Find it difficult to set limits.*

- *It is not clear to them how far is the reach of what they feel and where what the other feels begins.*

- *Take responsibility for the feelings of others.*

- *Their self-esteem is low.*

- *Since they don't feel good about themselves, they fear rejection.*

- *Are very helpful; always willing to help.*

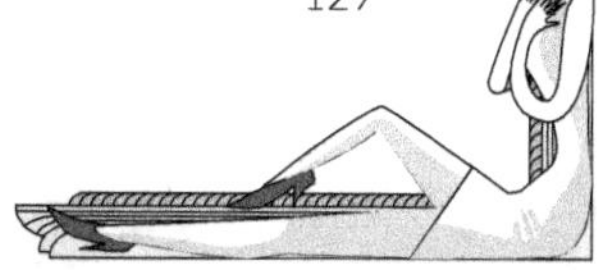

- *Seek the constant approval of the rest of the people.*

- *Justify the bad behavior of others.*

- *Are usually tolerant of abuse.*

- *Avoid confronting whoever is mean to them, justifying them.*

> Emotional codependency is not a good thing, it can even be very harmful. Codependents believe they are doing good while doing nothing but harming themselves and their environment.

& If we don't feel good about ourselves
and don't pay attention to ourselves,
we will never be able to properly care
an attend for others.

No confusion

There is another angle to looking at dependence that is softer and much more frequent. Sometimes, culture builds us by matching concepts that really have nothing to do with each other, for example:

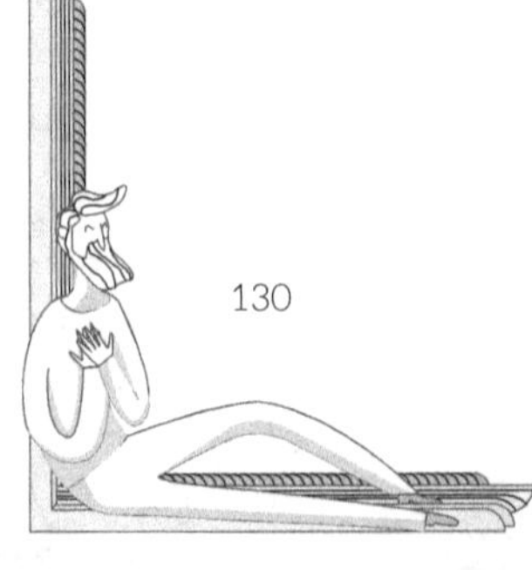

Nilda Chiaraviglio

All this hides very high costs:

- ⚜ *He who **sacrifices** himself is distracted from himself and becomes irresponsible for his own well-being.*

- ⚜ *It is common that he/she is waiting **in vain for** his/her **sleeplessness** and efforts to be rewarded.*

- ⚜ *Internal balance is sought through complaint, tantrums, blaming others, and judgment, and far from receiving attention, they receive rejection, threats of abandonment and contempt.*

- ⚜ *They become a person who stopped inspiring, nurturing, generating ideas or opportunities.*

- ⚜ *Isolation and loneliness arrive.*

- ⚜ *There is the threat of extinction of all the bonds that suffocate them.*

- ⚜ *The person who depends on another economically generates an existential doubt: will he be there because he chooses him or because it is impossible to leave?*

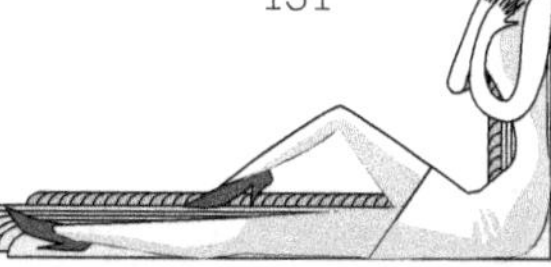

   The emotionally dependent person becomes a boring burden and will only serve to be used for what they know how to do.

   The person who depends sexually thinks that they lack their own pleasure, that it has to be given to them by another, then they will end up looking for someone who is full of their own pleasure instead of a bottomless barrel.

   The person who depends socially will always live with the fear of being abandoned by the one they serve, because they would be left without an affective network of human support.

& People treat us the same way we treat ourselves, so think about what you're doing with yourself.

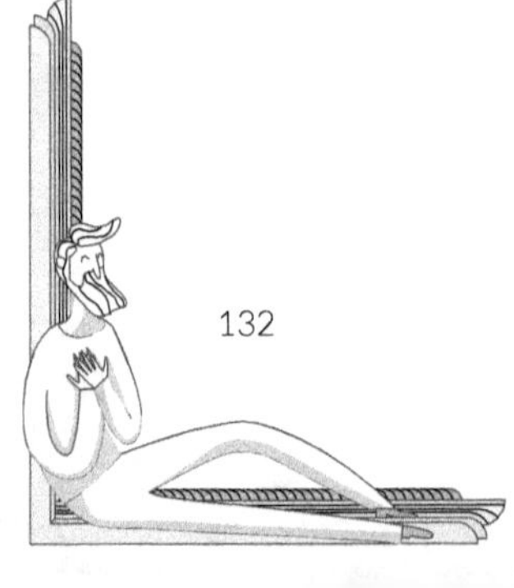

Nilda Chiaraviglio

Fact	Wrong interpretation
 If you think of yourself	You are selfish
 If you think of the other first	You are empathetic
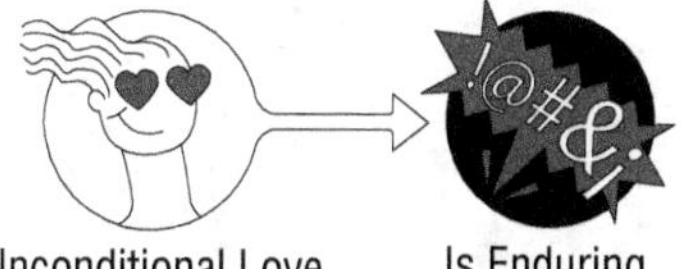 Unconditional Love	Is Enduring any mistreatment
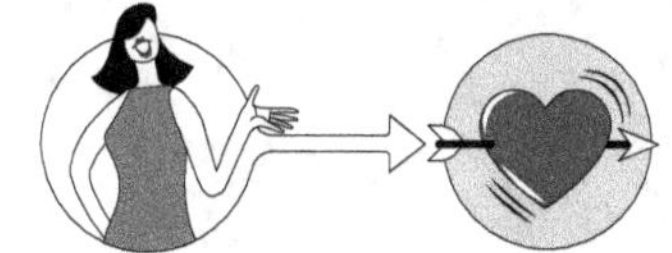 Always doing whatever the other proposes	Is synonymous of love
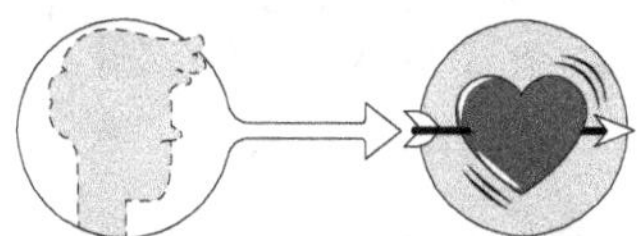 Blurring or erasing yourself	Is Love
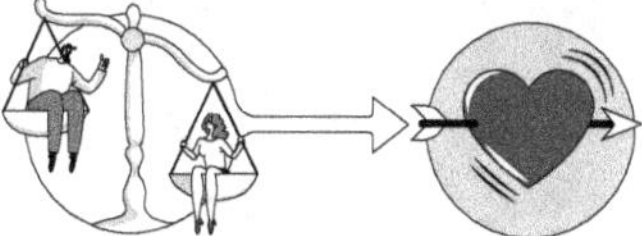 Postponing your Projects for those of the other	Is real Love

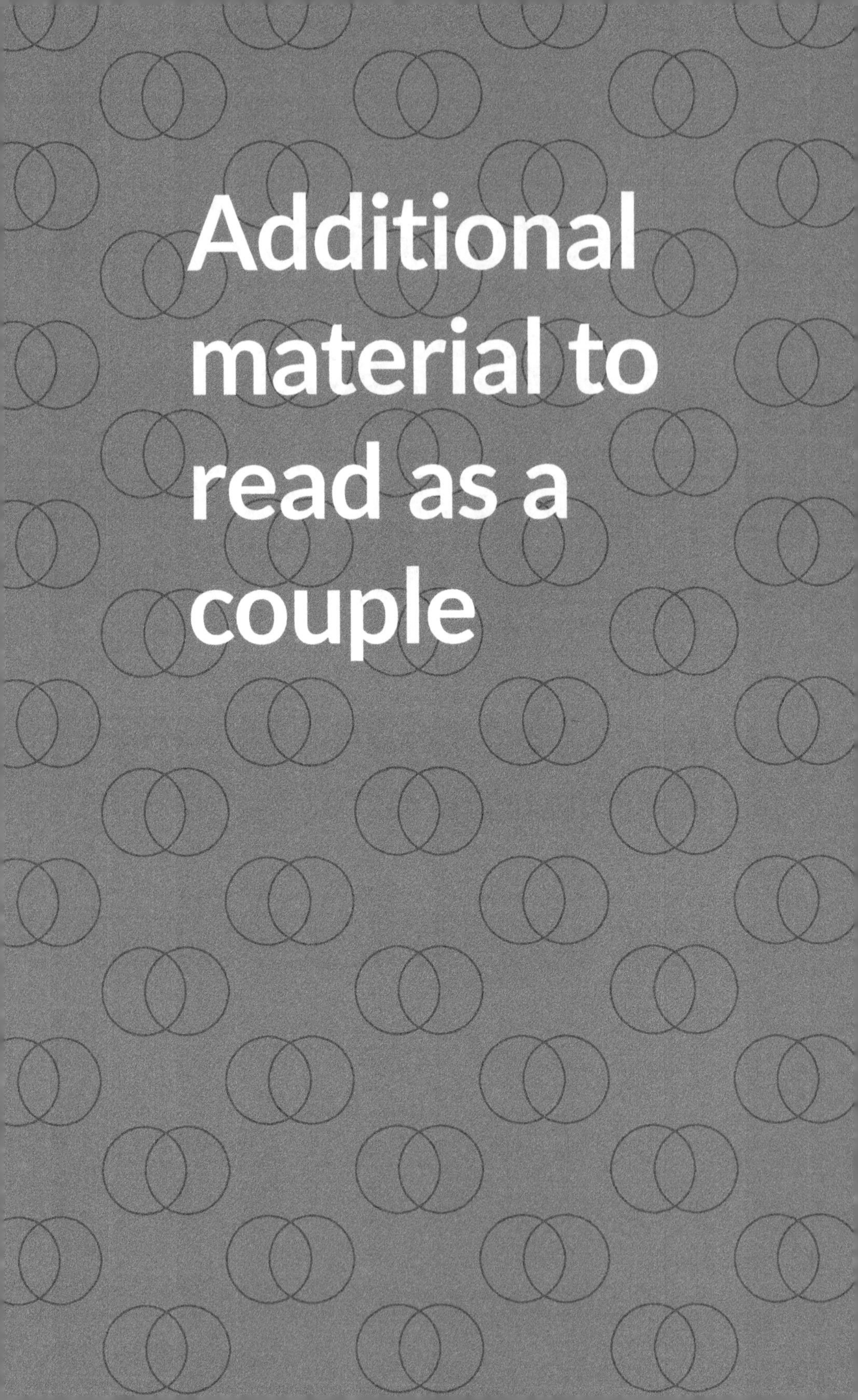

Additional
material to
read as a
couple

Paradigms of the Patriarchal Apocalypse

The patriarchal system in which we have lived for hundreds of years has inherited paradigms that have brought symptoms and consequences. It would be very useful for each person to reflect on what percentage of their life is built from these four Paradigms of the Apocalypse.

	HIERARCHY	CONFRONTATION
Meaning	I am your authority / I submit to you	I am right / You are right
Symptoms	Authoritarianism Dependencies Shame	Conflicts Fights Rupture of affective networks Superiority / Inferiority
Consecuences	Submissions and obstacles in mental, physical and emotional development	Impossibility of communication Invasion of other people's spaces
Price	Impotence and resentment Inability to set limits Destruction of eroticism and pleasure	Isolation and emotional problems Insecurities Pathologies in sexuality
Positive intention	**Setting boundaries that contain chaos and are healthy**	**Defining quality of life and choosing nurturing relationships**

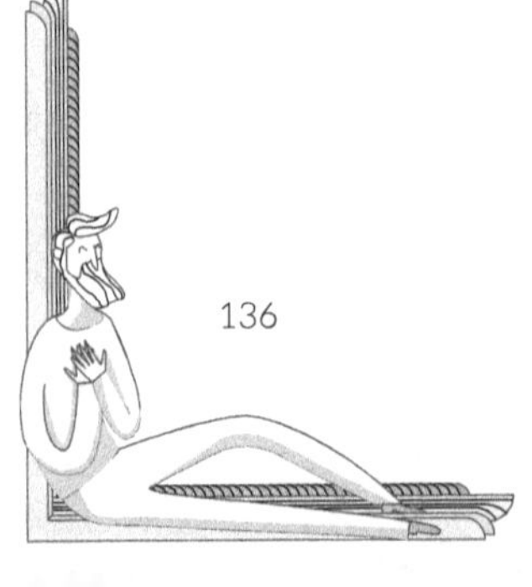

Nilda Chiaraviglio

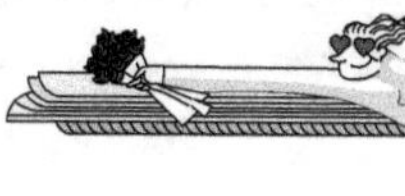

COMPETITION	EXCLUSION
I am more than you / I am less than you	Since what you think, feel, and do is different from mine, I discard you.
Imitation / Admiration Dependencies Irresponsibility Inadequacy and fear	Belief in a hostile world Jealousy Control Fear of abandonment Envy Abuses Guilt, resentment and revenge
Toxic relationships without respect	Rigidity Distrust Formation of institutions that collect destroyed people
Struggles for the need to win Alienating infatuation Exacerbation of power. Gender-based violence. Nullification of erotic love	Violence of all kinds Fanaticism, wars Exacerbation of political power Rejection of sexual diversity
Establishment of new goals and incentives for the evolution of the Being	Finding the right distances with each human relationship, without basing them on grudges

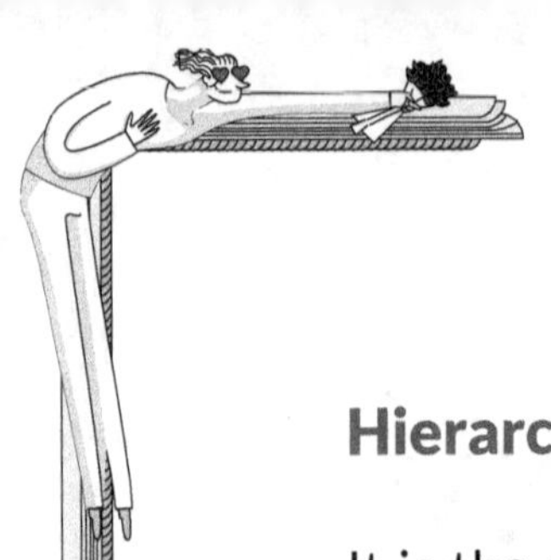

Hierarchy

It is the difference between authority (which is earned through conduct and constitutes us as an example) and authoritarianism («You will do as I say because I say so» and it is made clear that there will be reprisals if otherwise).

Authority is the space where we place ourselves in life based on our talents, not out of obligation; we are because it is the right thing to do and we want to learn from it, without the fear of punishment from whoever is issuing the instruction.

In the couple under the patriarchal paradigm, hierarchy is used as a form of domination of one of the members who imposes his will on the other, who decides to submit by cultural will and his capacity for development is limited to whatever the dominator allows. The concept of love is, «I'm going to make you happy at my expense».

Confrontation

It is when there is a conflict for the simple fact that someone wants to be right. It turns out that *REASON* does not exist, only "my reasons" and "yours" do, which are really "your interpretations" and "mine" about what happens out there. These interpreta-

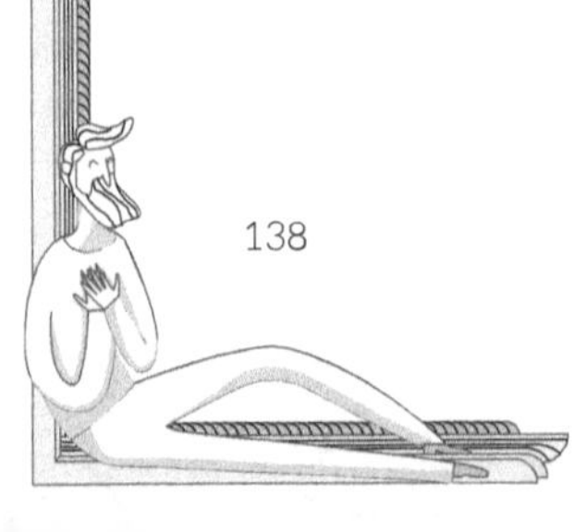

Nilda Chiaraviglio

tions are different for each person because they depend on the life history of each one. The answer is to listen with curiosity to each other's reasons, and create an **open dialogue** to enrich each other.

Competition

It is when one of the members of the couple feels that he is, has, knows or weighs more than the other. We all have different qualities or greater background in some subject: the greater that difference, it implies that someone wants to impose themselves, then violence appears. It's one thing to be competent and another to be competitive. It is one thing to say «I **can** be better every day» (I am responsible for my development) and another to think «I have to be better» (I compete **against** others).

Exclusion

Racism, religious intolerance and gender violence are some examples of exclusion: «If I don't agree with what you are or think, I discard you and the problem is over.» It is an accumulation of the other three paradigms. In romantic love, it is reflected in economic, emotional, sexual or social abuse, and is expressed in threats of abandonment, the decision to ignore the other, violence of all kinds, and so on.

Understand the romantic type of love of Hollywood, boleros, rancheras, tangos...

If we reflect on our pain, anger and discomfort, we will become aware that the patriarchal belief system is the root of the industrial mentality, the capitalist process of production and distribution of wealth, exploitation, and anxiety or fear of the future.

The development of generalized violence, through **Hierarchy**, **Confrontation**, **Competition** and **Exclusion** brings together the necessary characteristics to consolidate the dissatisfaction of human beings who will console themselves momentarily and circumstantially through the infinite growth of consumption, both of goods and of other human beings, all ephemeral and disposable.

In family structures there seems to be an obligation to love each other, regardless of what happens or fails to happen among its members. Thus, we observe overprotective , double bonded or absent mothers, authoritarian, punishing or unknown fathers, etc; who in any case must be loved and cared for in their old age because they contributed their eggs or sperm.

All this generates confusion when defining whether we love or are loved We can be immersed in the cycle of violence and justify that behavior «for the love that unites us».

When the expectations of eternal happiness are placed on a single person (the partner), an attachment to that affective dependency is generated, which becomes a series of more or less unattainable needs. When we ask out of necessity, we are willing to receive whatever others can give us: crumbs.

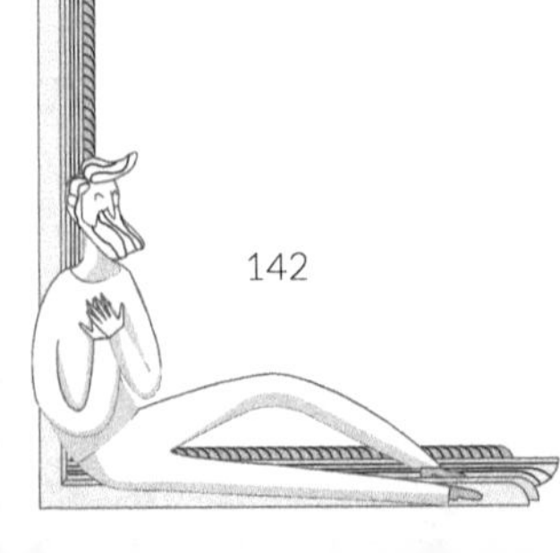

&   The accumulation of crumbs results in a miserable life, which only serves to suffer.The needs of this concept of romantic type of love and love–erotic relationship generate consequences such as:

Las necesidades que este tipo de concepto de amor romántico y de relación de pareja amoro-so-erótica genera consecuencias como:

&   *Individualism of a narcissistic nature.*

&   *The consumption of bodies and sexuality.*

&   *Disposable relationships.*

&   *Denial of all uncomfortable reality that would be a good idea to be thought about and reflected on.*

&   *Happiness through permanent fun.*

&   *Intensity as an expression of success, with substance use and abuse.*

&   *Beauty stereotypes.*

&   *Personal assesment through compliance with fashionable social canons.*

- *The permanent judgment of good and bad through whether it is valued or not by others.*

- *The division of emotions into positive and negative.*

- *The justification of any self-destructive behavior through fashions such as stress, anxiety, depression, low self-esteem, etc.*

- *The approach of unattainable ideals (magical thinking) as a source of frustration, confusion, submission and violence.*

- *Beliefs such as: «I am going to make you happy», «Love can achieve everything», «Enduring the unbearable means love", «I give my life for you», «I cannot live without you», etc.*

If we reflect on the concept of love and transform the idea of finiteness and magical thinking towards a concept of love as a human capacity in constant development, the patriarchal concept of affective relationship as private property also changes towards contextualized and growing relationships of individual freedom.

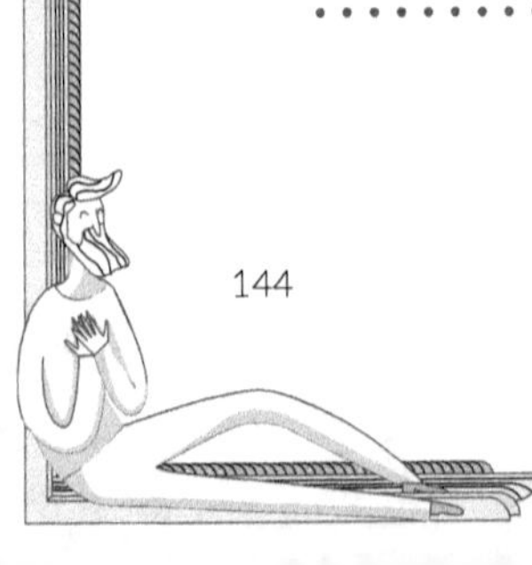

Nilda Chiaraviglio

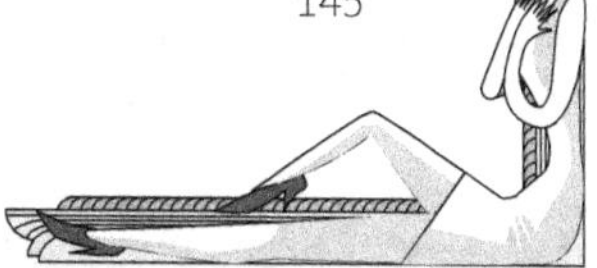

The gestation of the abuse affront violation

In our country, abuse is an everyday issue. Eight out of ten women —and seven out of ten men— suffer child sexual abuse. Perhaps, what outrages us the most is that 80% of these abuses happen within the framework of family and very close friends of the family.

    &   Abuse is one of the forms that violence takes in our culture, which is generated in all of us and by all of us, every single day..

The culture of silence

Let's talk once again about the patriarchal culture and its four paradigms. From the earliest childhood, we are educated to normalize violence through values grafted onto the paradigms of dominant hierarchy and exclusion.

To endorse the blows in formal education, both at home and at school, the horror stories that sow fear of life, mistrust, racism, sexism, anthropophagy, and normalized violence in children were classified as valuable educational instruments. We call them beautiful children's games and we forget that the creators of these double standard stories are the product of a time when children had to be terrorized with threats of all kinds.

& We multiply values that will be reproduced in adult life, unless we understand what we do and consciusly choose to weaken those discriminatory and harmful paradigms.

Abusers, but also many judges, police officers, prosecutors and public ministries, are traditionalist men and women who have been raised with stereo-typed sex roles, and then they reproduce them.

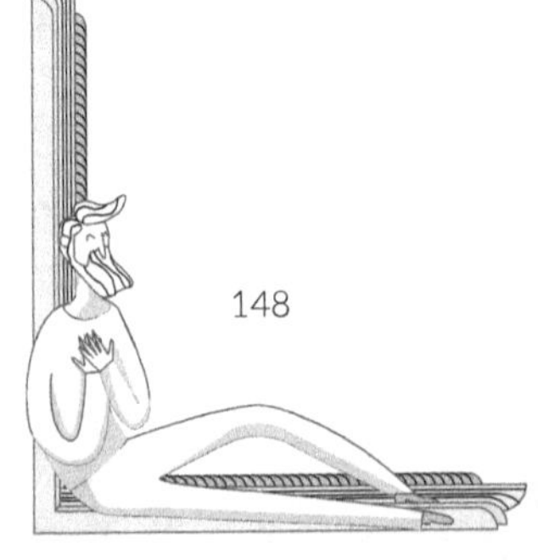

Nilda Chiaraviglio

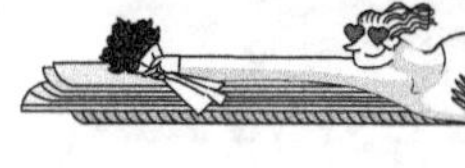

> There is a clear link between rape and the tendency of some men to possess, dominate and mistreat women and girls: 99% of rapes are perpetrated by men.

The normalization of sexual violence plays a critical role in silencing child abuse.

Sexual abuse and child pornography are scandalous products of a society that silenced its victims for hundreds of years.

There is another type of silence: when a girl or a boy has kept quiet for some time about the abuse of a pedophile and for some reason it is discovered and they manage to verbalize it, the first reaction on the part of the family is that of goshawk and disbelief. Adults' capacity for denial is infinite. The first obstacle that minors must overcome is that of their own environment.

> The capacity for denial is a human ability, a defense mechanism that consists of facing conflicts by denying their existence or their relationship or relevance with the subject, at least in the short term and until we are prepared to handle the emotional impact of what has been experienced.

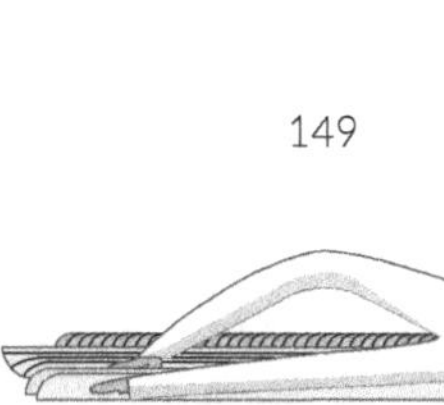

If we teach our children that our fragility is greater than theirs, even if they trust us, they will bear the guilt of asking us for help. It is one thing to show ourselves to be human with our family and quite another to place the heavy burden of our conflicts on them.

Today, there is a way to heal this type of trauma thanks to the neuroplasticity of the brain. All that is needed is the courage and commitment of the person who suffered that terrible outrage.

& Remember that silence is a big part of the problem.

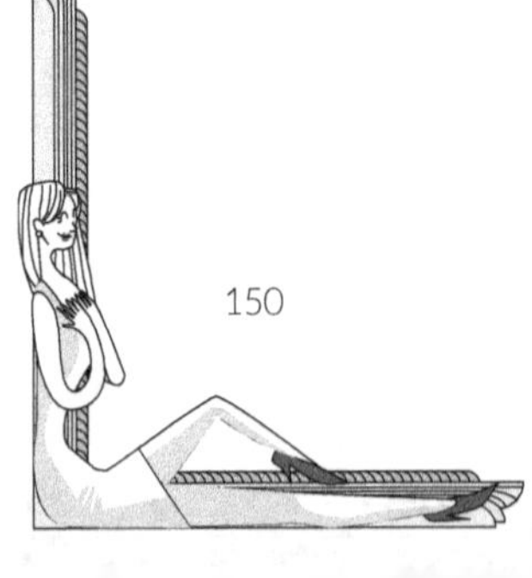

Special Thanks

To Bucky, the father of our daughters, with whom we built a beautiful family. During my relationship with him I became a lot of who I am today.

To the wonderful community of the diploma «El Placer de Amar», from which I nurture my self: You inspire me every day.

To my work team, thanks to which I extended the lands to sow my reflections, to cultivate the denaturalization of violence and the hope that «yes, you can and it is beautiful» to take responsibility for our own well-being in order to share it.

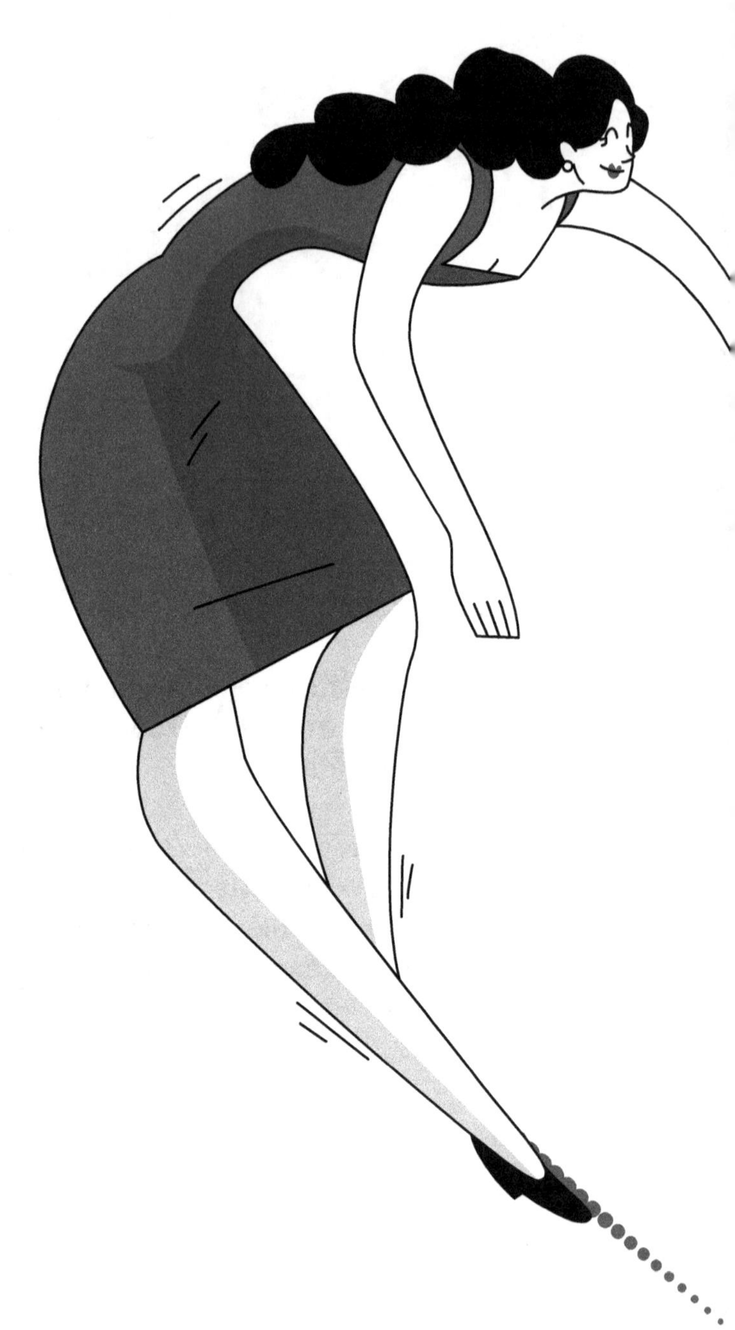

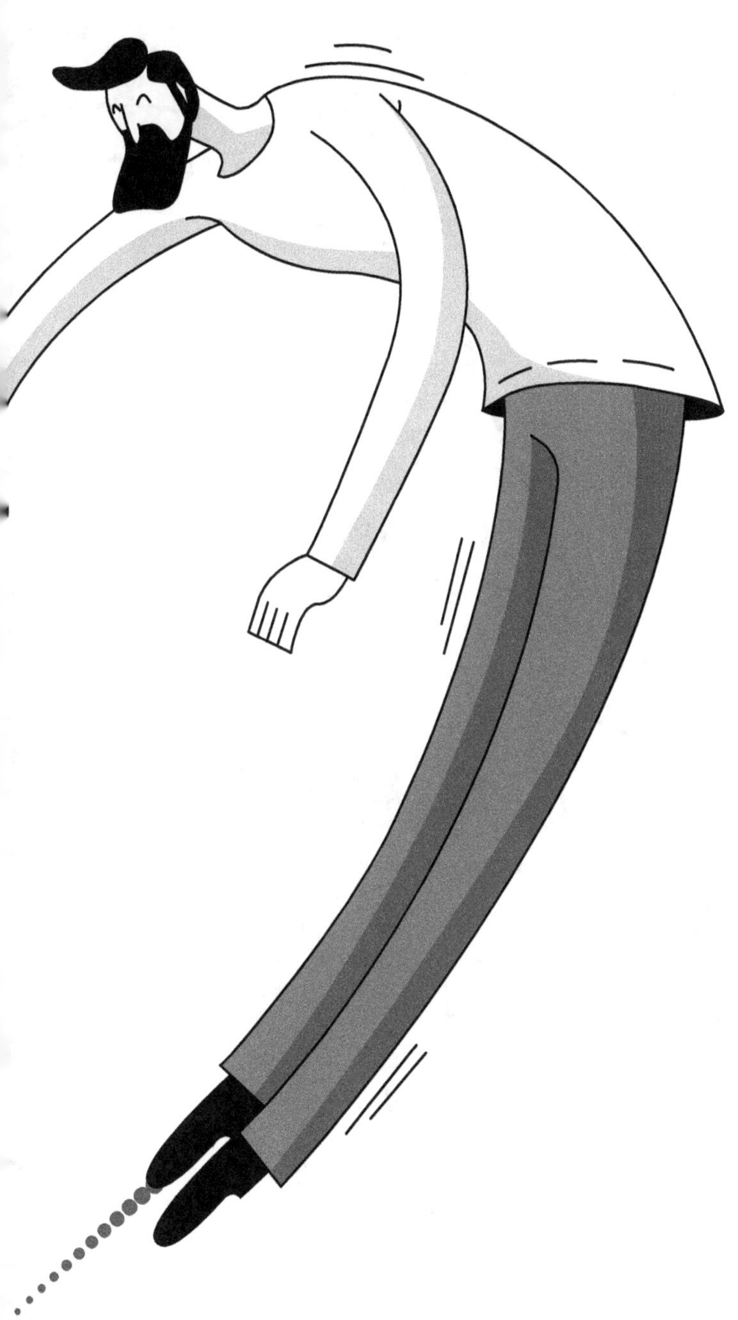